Fast Food Education

Calling for a more natural approach to teaching & learning in America

Dr. P. Mark Taylor
Darris J. Brock

Koinonia Associates LLC
Clinton, Tennessee

ISBN   978-1-60658-000-4

Published by:
Koinonia Associates LLC
Box 763
Clinton, TN 37717

To learn how you can become a published author, visit
http://www.KoinoniaAssociates.com

Dedication

This book is the culmination of many years of life experiences, much of which have been spent in schools. We love teaching. We love stirring students to make connections and think for themselves. This book is dedicated to all of those who share our passion for teaching and learning, to all of those who dedicate themselves to the development of the next generation. It is our sincere hope that this book will stimulate changes in schooling in the United States of America in a way that makes your lives richer.

A Note from the Authors

To enhance the flow of the book, we have attempted to meld our voices to speak as if we were one person. We only step out of this once near the end of chapter four, where we mention the different paths we have traveled that led us to reach the same conclusion.

CONTENTS

CHAPTER 1:
"OWED" TO SALLY

Sally was an average student. I knew that she was capable of thinking but was a reluctant participant in my Algebra 2 class. To be specific, Sally seemed to be most concerned with:

Surviving high school
Making sure her make-up and hair were just right
Talking to her friends
Avoiding speaking in class

More poignantly, Sally did not expect to understand the mathematics we were doing. She was merely hanging on to enough of it to escape with a low C.

On the last day of school, when the teaching and finals were all done, we were sitting around talking. Sally was relaxed and talking openly in a way that she had not done since the beginning of the school year. She turned her head a little and looked at me with an open and honest comment that cut me to the very core of my being: "Remember the first day of class when we did that lab with the bouncing balls? Yeah, I thought this class was going to be different." Ouch! I thought I had been different. I thought that I was doing a great job and I was a teacher that they could rely on to help them be ready for college and the rest of their lives but... BLAM! There it was. I had been revealed for the well-intended fraud that I was.

You see, on the first day of Algebra 2, I had the students working in groups of four. Each group was to drop a rubber ball and record the number of bounces. For each height we tried, they dropped the ball twice and counted the number of bounces. They recorded the average of the two for each height in an x-y table of values. Of course the balls were bouncing everywhere.

At times it looked a lot more like recess at a pre-school than an organized, purposeful lesson in an Algebra 2 class. Much of the time, the students needed more than two drops from a height for various reasons: the students counting were not ready, they were not sure that they had dropped it from the right height, ... but after one day of ball dropping and a second day of graphing and analyzing the results, they had learned. They understood from the results of dropping balls that not everything comes out to be linear. They understood that there were experiences in their lives that could be explained and predicted through higher mathematics.

They also understood that mathematics learning did not have to be boring.

Sally had learned this lesson well enough to know that we had spent the remainder of the year doing the drudgery of lecture and practice when there was a way that was more fun AND, more importantly, more meaningful. Sally's comment on the last day of Algebra 2 hit the nail on the head. While I had managed to teach many children a lot of mathematics, this unmotivated student had been more insightful and reflective than any comment that I had managed to utter during that school year.

SALLY'S PLACE IN MY LEARNING PROCESS

This experience reignited the flickering flame of my own learning process. Until this point, I had been haphazardly adding to my learning through experiences that came to me: by attending conferences that were suggested by colleagues, by answering questions that were asked of me by administrators, fellow teachers, or students, etc. About a year earlier I had been to a regional conference of the National Council of Teachers of Mathematics and been re-exposed to a fact that I had picked up as an undergraduate – there is a better way to teach, a way that leads to better learning for all students and helps students make sense out of the mathematics rather than merely memorizing facts and procedures.

It reminded me of the first time that I had heard about this strange new world of teaching and learning. It was as an undergraduate in the teacher education program at a small college in the middle of Missouri. There were only six education majors in the class of 1989 and I was the only future mathematics teacher in the bunch. As a result, only one of my courses actually dealt with mathematics teaching-- a one hour seminar. As I signed up for the course, I was bored out of my mind with the general education courses. While the content was new to me and offered insight into teaching in general, I was really excited by the idea that I would finally be studying mathematics teaching. After all, I had signed up to teach mathematics and until I got to mathematics, nothing seemed to be relevant. When I finally got to day one of the course, I found that the format was simple: the instructor would have either given me an article or have me look one up and read it. I would summarize the article and reflect on it and then we would meet for one hour each week to discuss it. That was it. No lecture. No lesson as far as I could see. Just read and discuss. I learned enough in the course to know that there was more out there, but at the end of the course I had no idea how to go about teaching that way. As a result, I started my student teaching experience doing to others as my teachers had done to me. This "traditional" method of teaching mathematics was captured as an idealized way of teaching by Madeline Hunter: anticipatory set, teaching, guided practice, independent practice, and closure. (I'll say more on that in chapter 2.)

By the time that Sally dropped her bomb on me, I had reached some level of mastery of this kind of teaching. After earning two college degrees in mathematics and seven years of teaching experience, including two. years as a teaching assistant in the mathematics department at a major university, I had reached the point that I was recognized as a dedicated and effective mathematics teacher by my principals, by my colleagues, and even by former students. In one painful and insightful moment, Sally had managed to put things in perspective. I was about as good as I was going to get at this kind of teaching. There was a better way to do it, however, and I needed to know how to get to it. Although I had been to a few conferences and read a few things that had reminded me of this, none of these seemed to help me overcome my old image of mathematics teaching. I came to the conclusion that after years of trying to overhaul the engine (my ideas about mathematics teaching and learning), what I needed was new car! I needed to have the old image of mathematics teaching completely replaced by a better model. I needed brain surgery!

FROM TEACHER TO TEACHER EDUCATOR

At this point, I quit my job as a high school teacher and went into graduate school to complete my doctorate in education and solve these dilemmas:

- How do we effectively teach mathematics to everyone, including the Sallys as well as the high achievers?

- How do we support teachers in their process of learning to teach that way so that not everyone needs to earn a PhD to figure it out?

Since that critical comment from Sally, I have spent five years on my Ph.D. at the University of Missouri (one at St. Louis, and four at Columbia, MO) and another seven years as a professor at the University of Tennessee in Knoxville. I have been an active participant in the research community focused on mathematics learning and mathematics teacher learning: doing research, presenting results at conferences, publishing the results in peer-reviewed journals, and even editing some publications. I have taught future mathematics teachers as undergraduates and graduates, taught graduate courses in mathematics education, and created a course called "Research Trends in Mathematics Teacher Education." As a professor in a doctoral program, I have even educated people on how to educate future teacher educators. Did you keep track of that? Take a look at the diagram below:

"Owed to Sally"

Dr. Taylor - (Me)	Mr. Parker - (Suzie's student)
• At the University of Tennessee - I taught future professors of matheamtics education like Tommy Hodges how to teach future professors about how to teach teachers.	• After learning about mathematics teaching from Dr. Ortiz, Mr. Parker goes on to a job at a high school and teaches Samantha mathematics in geometry course.

Dr. Hodges (My student at UT)	Dr. Ortiz - (Tommy's student)
• After learning about educating future professors of mathematics education, the new Dr. Hodges goes on to a big university and teaches Suzie Ortiz about mathematics teacher education.	• After learning about educating future and current teachers from Dr. Hodges, the new Dr. Suzie Ortiz goes on to another college and teaches Billy Parker how to teach mathematics to high school students.

I have had the honor of working with many great mathematics teachers, graduate students, colleagues in school districts, colleges and universities, and government officials. Through all of the various scholarly efforts, courses, and projects, I have stayed grounded by focusing on these two questions from a practical standpoint. At some point in the middle of these experiences I came to the obvious yet profound conclusion that teachers and students are both people, merely differing in roles. As such, the two questions have evolved into one:

How do people learn?

Moreover, how can we support that learning while respecting their individual goals in their various roles (parents, students, teachers, bankers, retirees, etc.) and contexts (schools, universities, businesses, government, etc.)?

ABOUT THIS BOOK

This book represents my current thinking on these questions as I have finally converged on a basic truth about learning that is much more powerful than I could have ever imagined: *People can teach themselves far better than they can be taught.* If it is that simple, why is a book necessary? The way that we educate people leads them away from learning the way that they learn best. In order to make that point in a way that is understandable, we have compared the way we handle knowledge in our culture to the way we handle food. Everybody understands food, right? In chapter two, we explore the relationship between the developments of formal education in America to the rise of fast food empires. In chapters three, four, and five, we go about our version of brain surgery: replacing the old image of formal education with an image of what it means to learn in a natural, healthy way that leads to success for more students. In chapters six and seven, we look at the same image of learning and the implications for educating future teachers as well as retooling those already teaching. In chapter eight, we examine the implications for schools, school districts, and for the entire educational system in terms of how to support learning of teachers and students. We then close with a word of caution.

Here is another story to convince you to keep reading:

A Man Crying about Elementary Mathematics:
While I was working on my doctoral degree at the
University of Missouri, my kids were starting their
school careers at Derby Ridge Elementary. Paul
Trafton, a well-known researcher in mathematics
education once told me that Derby Ridge "is a great
place to be a kid" because they allow students to
develop their own reasoning rather than imposing
reasoning on them. An emotional "Math Night" for
parents told me that Paul was right. As a Project
Construct school, the teachers had been formally
introduced to ways of teaching that harnessed
students' natural learning processes.

As we entered the meeting a few minutes late, I
looked around at the faces throughout the room and
saw that they were filled with tension. The teachers
were explaining how they were handling math
differently, not as a set of facts to be memorized but
as a process of making sense out of quantities and
shapes. One of their examples was in figuring the
sums of two-digit numbers:

$$\begin{array}{r} 25 \\ +37 \\ \hline \end{array}$$

They talked about the methods of adding where
you think in terms of familiar numbers and adding
parts that make sense. Since we often think in terms
of money, for instance, it is natural to think in terms
of quarters or 25's. Hence, one way to do this
problem is to think of 37 as 25 (a quarter) + 12 (12
more cents). Doing so means that you can think of 25
+ 37 as being 25 + (25 +12). We quickly know that
25+25 is 50 because it represents two quarters. So,

we can look at 25+37 as two quarters with 12 cents more or 50+12 which is 62. Since 12 cents is automatically thought of by many folks as a dime and two pennies, they may see this as a quarter plus a quarter, a dime, and two pennies. If we actually had this problem in our hands, we move the quarters together and decide that we have 50+10+2, which is 62. While there were several ways of adding mentioned at this meeting, one well-dressed fellow stood up and expressed concern that his child was not being taught the traditional algorithm: lining up the numbers and adding the ones first, carrying the tens, and then adding to get the solution. The teachers tried to talk their way through the research on it but it did not seem to move this man or several others that were in agreement with him.

Finally, the tension was broken by a parent that had a rather different emotionally charged response: "I want to thank you," he said to the teachers, his eyes welling with tears. "I have always done my arithmetic this way but my teachers told me that it was wrong so I had to hide it. I did it my way and then figured out how to write it their way so that I would be counted as getting it right." Fighting back an all-out cry, he talked about how he had felt ashamed that he did not think the way they wanted him to do. His last comment was simple and brought things home for me in a way that I will always remember: "I am a successful businessman and I do mathematics every day, not the way that my teachers told me, but the way they told me was wrong. The way you are teaching our kids is the way that I have been hiding for thirty years. Thank you."

This man was effective and efficient in the way that he did arithmetic on a daily basis. After all this time, he felt relieved. He had been freed from the burden that his teachers had placed on him and he could now feel free to openly discuss his reasoning with people. How is it that good mathematics (natural thinking processes that are correct and efficient) can go punished and memorizing without understanding (a lazy and unnatural approach to learning) can be rewarded? Unfortunately, this kind of teaching is more often the rule than the exception. Let's take a look at how this kind of unnatural learning has developed into being the norm in formalized education in the United States of America.

According to standardized testing, we are gradually getting better over time. The National Assessment of Educational Progress (NAEP) has been collecting data for decades. More people are proficient at reading, mathematics, and science than ever before. The claim here is not that things are getting worse in terms of achievement but that things were never all that good in the first place. The progress documented through NAEP is good but it represents the tweaking of a system that is fatally flawed and has been since its inception. Contrary to popular belief, the problems in "modern education" have not occurred overnight. They have not evolved just over the last decade or two or even the last two generations. The problems stem from so far back that Mark Twain identified the same problems that haunt us today. Twain acknowledged the inconsistencies of formalized education and the natural way of learning in several instances:

"Education is what is left when you forget all the facts that your teacher made you memorize when you where in school."
"Education consists mainly in what we have unlearned."
"Don't let schooling interfere with your education."

The typical student in school or college today has drawn pretty much the same conclusion as Twain: school is unnatural and irrelevant. Make no mistake, they know the "right" answers – it is good for my future – it helps me to know stuff – it will help me get into college – it will help me get a good job. At the same time, students do not see direct connections between what they are learning in school and what they will do on the job. Moreover, if you ask the typical high school mathematics teacher how the content of their courses help the student they may be able to list general fields, but they can rarely tell you specifically where any one skill learned in their class will be applied by their students in the future. The truth is that they may not see any of it in the future. It is not that mathematics is not useful but that the version of mathematics taught in schools is not useful. I had a poster hanging on the wall in my high school mathematics classroom that charted specific mathematics skills to specific jobs. It was my attempt to by-pass the frequent question that students ask: "When are we ever going to use this in real life?" When they would ask the question, I would point to the wall and say, "Find it!" While it worked for those that were extremely goal-oriented, it backfired strongly for many. They would simply say, "Yes, but I am not going to do any of those jobs. Why do I have to know this? Can I just go to the library and read while the people that actually need to learn this work on it?" How do you argue with that? So it is with much of the K-12 and college curriculum. I have never had to answer questions on short stories in the real world, how about you?

HOW INSTEAD OF WHAT

Although the students' questions tend to focus on what is taught, perhaps the real question should be about how it is taught. The literature teacher would talk about things like understanding "the human condition" or "understanding the power of stories." The mathematics teacher will talk about the value of learning "how to think logically" as a benefit of their courses. These things are important, even critical, to individual success and to the success of our nation, but the way they are approached is crucial.

Simply answering questions about short stories and factoring trinomials are not activities that lead to a deep knowledge or the kind of critical thinking skills that the teachers would like to claim. The high-level thinking that could emerge out of exploring short stories and quadratic functions is all too often lost in the process. The most important goals that could be worked on are not what is being emphasized in the lessons. Briefly stated, the real content (how to think your way through mathematically or how to communicate and/or understand human issues) is often overshadowed and frequently replaced by the delivery mechanisms (factoring quadratics and answering questions about short stories). This flawed delivery mechanism is what takes an important, natural education and reduces it to an unnatural education that must eventually be supplanted when a student engages in life after formal education.

CHAPTER 2:
EDUCATIONAL PROGRESS
AND FAST FOOD

There are natural consequences to an unnatural education. The business community has numerous complaints about the kind of young people that it is forced to hire. There still remains a large portion of students who do not graduate from high school. Beyond the issue of illiteracy, however, lurks innumeracy. Even young people who successfully graduate from high school often can't think themselves through quantitative situations and need more education after high school. The most famous example of corporations dealing with these issues is McDonalds. In the 90's, McDonald's installed cash registers that figure the change so that the person working the register would not have to subtract in order to figure out what change to give back to the customer. Colleges are fighting similar battles. At your local community college you can find as many as six math courses that students can take before they get to college level mathematics. None of those six courses count toward any degree program. They are simply re-teaching high school math. But the vast majority of those students got B's and C's on high school math on the same content. So what's going on?

Another complaint of business people is the inability of college graduates to collaborate. Those that they hire straight out of college have no idea how to work together. Up to that point, the best students have been competitive rather than collaborative. In fact, a frequent complaint of high quality students comes when they are forced to work with a group. The fear is that the work of the group will not be of the quality which the student typically generates. Despite this complaint, collaboration is one of the most important attributes that an employer needs. The story of one particular Ph.D. professor will illustrate this problem.

This professor came onto the campus and wanted to insert himself in the school system. To that end, he worked with another professor teaching a related course until such a time as his colleague was put in charge over both courses. At that time he stopped all collaboration and seldom even answered e-mails with questions or suggestions from the other professor. His desire was not to work together but to dominate. This was true to the education process as he had experienced it: competitive rather than collaborative. He had never worked in the real world and had never developed the collaborative skills necessary for good corporate collaboration.

There is a misconception that as you climb the ladder you become less and less accountable to others and you expect more and more autonomy. My kids think that way all the time. "I'm grown up. I don't have to talk to you about that stuff. I'm big," is the typical line of thinking. In fact, the complete opposite is true. The higher you climb up the ladder the more people you are accountable to and the more you have to collaborate.

How has the educational system evolved to the point where logically sound and practical thinking is squished out of students early and standardized snippets of knowledge are memorized? To get a better idea, compare the development of traditional educational methods, a prepackaged knowledge and its delivery system, to the development of prepackaged foods and their delivery systems. These distinctly different topics are frighteningly parallel in their development, in the problems inherent in such systems, and in the methods of overcoming problems.

Junk Food Hangover: My friend Gary is a body builder. It is what he does for a living. Gary once told me that six days a week he eats perfectly. He eats only basic foods, foods as close to the way they were grown in nature as possible. He prepares them himself doing the least amount of cooking as possible.

Finally, he eats the basic foods that he has prepared in a specific order to maximize the benefits. According to Gary, you are supposed to eat the protein first because it takes the longest to digest, starches/carbohydrates next, and veggies last because they have roughage and they clean your body out after it is finished digesting the nutrients that it needs from the rest of the food. On Sundays, however, Gary would eat anything he felt like eating. He would hit McDonalds like it was going out of business. Big Macs, candy bars, ice cream, whatever sounded good was good enough. On Mondays, however, his head hurt, his body didn't move as well as it should, and he was generally cantankerous. He had a fast-food hangover. He absolutely loved the pleasures of fast-food Sundays, but every Monday he realized how bad he had been. His body ached because it was rejecting that which was unnatural.

HOOKED ON FAST-FOOD

Most of us do not eat healthily enough to recognize when we are experiencing a fast-food hangover. In fact, a large percentage of Americans live in that state. According to a story on http://www.cbsnews.com, "Every day nearly one-third of U.S. children aged 4 to 19 eat fast food, which likely packs on about six extra pounds per child per year and increases the risk of obesity, a study of 6,212 youngsters found." In an excerpt from the book *Good Stuff?* posted on worldwatch.org, the author states the following facts about the global spread of food uniformity:

- At many fast-food restaurants, a single meal gives a disproportionate share—sometimes more than 100 percent—of the recommended daily intake of fat, cholesterol, salt, and sugar.
- In the United States, an estimated 65 percent of adults are overweight or obese, leading to an annual loss of 300,000 lives and to at least $117 billion in health care costs in 1999.
- A recent study showed that children who drink sodas and other sugar-sweetened drinks are more often obese and that this risk increases another 60 percent with each additional beverage consumed.

The fact that we Americans are living longer lives than our ancestors doesn't mean we are healthier. We merely live with more complications. Have you looked into the medicine cabinet of the average 65 year old? It can be a frightening experience. According to the Families USA web site, (http://www.familiesusa.org) the average number of prescriptions per elderly person grew from 19.6 in 1992 to 28.5 in 2000, an increase of 45 percent.

By 2010, the average number of prescriptions per elderly person is projected to grow to 38.5, an increase of 10 prescriptions, or 35 percent, per senior since 2000.

From 1992 to 2010, the average number of prescriptions per senior will grow by 96 percent.

The overall total number of prescriptions for seniors grew from 648 million in 1992 to over 1 billion in the year 2000—and is projected to grow to almost 1.6 billion in 2010.

Those are the statistics for the generation that did not start eating fast food until later in life. What will they be like for the children that are sucking down sodas and going back for free refills on their way out?

While we have all heard the truth about the slow poisoning of our bodies through fast food, we are reluctant to believe that these facts apply to us. "It doesn't FEEL bad, after all. It gives me energy. I pay attention to the calories and eat salads part of the time. Isn't that good?"

Why do we cling so tightly to that which makes us feel so lousy? Simple. If you have forgotten what healthy feels like, it might be natural to think that the problems with fast-food are being overstated; that it is just not as bad as people say. WRONG! It is merely another case of the boiled frog syndrome. If you put a frog into boiling water it will jump out, but if you put a frog into comfortable water and slowly turn up the heat it will be content to stay and end up boiled. Likewise, if you feed a healthy person fast-food it will make him sick, but if you feed an unhealthy person fast food he may not notice or may even feel better for a short time. Gary noticed the difference every week because he did not allow himself to get used to the bad feeling.

How have so many Americans gotten used to feeling poorly as a way of life? One step at a time.

Let's look at the last century:

Late 1800s to Early 1900s
 What: Industrial Revolution
 How : Mass production via assembly line
 Where: Workplace moves from home to factories
 Impact on food: More people rely on grocery
 stores

1915-1948
 What: World Wars & Great Depression
 How: Dads work for government & Moms go to work
 Where: More families move to cities
 Impact on food: More people rely on grocery
 stores & restaurants

1949-1988
 What: Urban Sprawl
 How: Lower prices for cars as well as more and better roads
 Where: Middle class moves to the suburbs
 Impact on food: More people rely on
 standardized groceries (TV dinners, microwave
 meals,...) and the growing fast food &
 standardized restaurant industries

STATUS OF FOOD AS OF 2008

Home cooking: After 30 years of microwave ovens
and pizza delivery in thirty minutes or less, even

home cooking is rarely done at home. Salads come pre-packaged in bags, just rinse and serve. Meals are cooked at the grocery store; just pick it out, take it home, and serve it on paper plates.

<u>Restaurants</u>: Over half a century after Ray Kroc and Colonel Sanders standardized burgers and fried chicken, a large percentage of restaurants are standardized. Drive to any town in America. The closer you get to the mall, the more familiar the restaurants become. You can go to your favorite restaurant, order your favorite items, and expect it to taste exactly the same. Whether it is Cracker Barrel, McDonald's, or Chili's, you know exactly what to expect. You can even get your favorite Starbucks coffee in locations around the world!

All of these represent the best of standardized food. As we mentioned before, however, the price we are paying for this convenience and familiarity is our health. The real problem with standardized food, however, is the standards themselves. They are measured by speed and the degree to which they make the consumer happy for the moment. This leads to high fructose corn syrup in the French fries and free refills on sodas that are around 250 calories per refill. The idea of standardizing food is not bad. The problem is that it is measured and standardized using the wrong standards. If standardized foods were all required to be healthy foods with reasonable portions, no doctor would need to ask a patient to stop eating them. Personally, my absolute favorite standardized restaurant meal weighs in at 1,850 calories. That is without catsup, honey-mustard sauce, or the soda that adds about 250 calories per free refill. That is more calories than most people actually need in an entire day!

SO WHAT DOES THIS HAVE TO DO WITH LEARNING?

The development of standardized learning over the last century is very similar to the development of standardized food. As the industrial revolution evolved, changing the structure of families and daily work, it became clear that more children should be in school. The mandatory school attendance laws in many states were first put into effect between 1870 and 1910. This is the time when more folks were moving together into large communities surrounding factories. Parents were spending more time in their factories which, assuming the children were not working in the factories, meant that these parents were spending less time with their children. As a result, the apprenticeship model that was the dominant model of education since the beginning of time was beginning to fade. As the decades moved on, more and more of the children in America were going to school.

Gearing up for more children created a need for streamlining the educational process. It also meant that more rigorous and standardized processes needed to be in place. If the state governments were going to require education, then schools would have to become more standardized. The lack of such standards was having a negative impact on colleges, so a committee was appointed and operated in the 1890's to address the issue. One of the ideas set forth by this committee was the concept that later became known as the Carnegie unit, the unit that measures progress in high schools still today. It represents the first step towards standardization of the high school curriculum in the United States.

THE ASSEMBLY LINE

To be sure, standardization in the schools was a good idea. It was the implementation that went awry. The model for schooling reflected the changing times. With Henry Ford's success in mass production, the assembly line was the best invention since sliced bread. More automobiles were being cranked out with more speed, more efficiency, and lower cost. The principle is simple: have one employee do the same thing to every car. One employee. One job. Niche specialization. Each automobile would reach the worker's station in exactly the same stage of completion and each would leave the worker with exactly the same work being done. In this way, less decision-making is needed and more action is accomplished. Applied to education, however, this meant that schools began to operate in a similar way; the children were being grouped by age to make the process more manageable. Even the rural schools began to move from the one-room school-house model. What is wrong with this, you may ask? Only one thing: age is the wrong standard by which to determine a student's readiness to move to the next stage in the assembly line. As with fast food, children's educational completeness is being measured by the wrong standard. In food preparation, an item moves to the next stage of assembly when the product is completely done with the content of that station. If it is the condiment station, then it gets all the appropriate condiments before moving on to add the beef patty.

In terms of education, what was the measure being used to move a "product' to the next stage on the assembly line? Since school is supposed to be about learning, one would expect that the item being measured to determine a child's readiness to move on to the next work station (grade level) in this assembly line (schooling system) would be how much they have learned. While grades are used as a way to keep a few students from progressing, it is age and the passage of time that are the primary measuring sticks. Imagine that a major auto manufacturer had decided that they would move an auto to the next stage of the assembly line as long as the work was at least 65% complete. Would you want to drive their cars? For that matter, at what percent of completion would you like the standard to be set for the manufacturing of your next car? Worse yet would be the scenario of social promotion: since we do not want the cars to feel bad, we will keep moving them down the line even though they are not even 65% completed.

Now imagine that some autos are coming to the work station with that particular manufacturing task (third grade, for instance) 100% completed. Are they moved on to the next stage? No! You have to leave them there and tweak them until the time is up and only then can they be moved on. What a waste of time! This is what happens to students in our schools that are extremely capable and high-achieving. They are placed in "honors" or "gifted" programs but they are not moved on to the next phase of education (next course, next grade level, etc.). What a waste! Is it any wonder that so many talented students believe school is mostly a waste of time!

High schools took the assembly line concept to a new level. The content and the process were both deeply impacted by the work of the NEA Committee of Ten in the 1890s along with the introduction of the assembly line. The idea of having credits in high school toward graduation, Carnegie units, was an idea of this committee. The work of the committee was extensive and the report came out over several years. As people began to understand the assembly line concept, Carnegie units became popular. Just like assembly lines, the end result was division of labor. An effort was made to compartmentalize the content that is learned in high school. What was learned in one course was clearly separated from what you learned in another course, divided by the clear boundaries of the credit. This was a bit of a contradiction, however, because one of their recommendations was to integrate math and science.

While it may be necessary to some degree to have teachers become niche specialists, we have all heard stories about people so focused on their particular slice of education that they are unable to relate to other areas. That communicates loudly and clearly to the students that they should store these ideas from mathematics, science, English, and social studies all in different silos in their brains. Whenever I ask mathematics students to write, they tend to moan and complain about it. "This is not English!" Writing in full sentences, paragraphs, and essays about the mathematics that they have learned, however, forces students into the position of organizing their thoughts, therefore reinforcing what they have learned. Sometimes, it even gives them a chance to correct their own wrong thinking.

Another assembly line feature of the high school was the use of resources in terms of time, space, and teachers. A student was moved from one work station (classroom) to the next several times a day until they were done for that day. This process was to be repeated for many days and then a new schedule is constructed at either the semester break or at the end of the school year. In this way, the product, an education, was developed. This also has the natural consequence of students' tendency to see courses and years of school as being in separate compartments. Students may learn the content to the satisfaction of their teacher in 7th grade and then move off to 8th grade having put it behind them. Often when expected to know something from the previous year, the students will claim that they have never seen that idea before. This makes it interesting for teachers such as my aunt. At one point, she was the only mathematics teacher for grades 7 through 12 in a very small school district. As with all kids, her students would claim that they had never learned it but she knew they had. She could tell them when they learned it and what grade they earned on the test over it.

We have standardized, compartmentalized, and pre-packaged learning in such a structured environment that there is no room for autonomy; no room for having your own questions, the kind of learning we enjoy so much! When we have a question, we get excited about learning. If we are not allowed to engage our curiosity, education is reduced to a game to beat. The problem is not that students aren't thinking. On the contrary, their minds are very busy. The problem is that they are trying to answer the wrong question. Unmotivated students will ask, "How do I get out of working?" They will work for hours to avoid minutes of work. The work they do is not productive in the eyes of the teacher and is certainly counterproductive for the students' own good. The most productive students ask, "How can I get the best possible grade with all of these classes and band practice?" It is not that the minds of these students are lazy. On the contrary, they are always at work. The problem is simply that young minds will not be tamed. They must engage in asking questions and finding answers. This assembly line system of schooling, however, discourages them from inquiring about the things that matter.

SCHOOL AS A SOCIAL PROGRAM

The responsibility of feeding a family used to be on the entire family. If they wanted meat, dad went out and killed it. If they wanted bread, they worked in the field for months to grow the wheat. As the culture shifted, the responsibility shifted. Now the work of finding and preparing food is nearly entirely on the shoulders of strangers, often many miles away. Hence, fast food is also lazy food. Likewise, there has been a shift in responsibility that has moved towards a similar work ethic in learning. Culturally, some historical events impacted this shift significantly. In the 1930's, the U.S. government began to provide for the people rather than the other way around. Social programs abounded that paid for a family's food and provided a structured way to provide for their future as well through social security. As more people began to see the government as their caretaker, more people began to see the public schools as social programs as well. As time went on, social promotions outweighed the need to achieve a certain level before moving to a higher grade. The war years moved the idea of schools as a social program to a new level. People began to see school as the place that children develop their social skills, interaction patterns, and morals.

This pattern of social activism through public education is still seen in 2008. Extreme physical development through sports team participation, behavioral management and moral development (Whose morals are being taught is a book unto itself.), as well as academic achievement are now seen as rights that must be granted by the schools. A school that does not somehow transform a child into a successful individual can expect to be sued for this travesty of justice despite the spiraling decrease in parent involvement and the lack of motivation by the child. In 1880, the responsibility for educational achievement was firmly on the child and his parents, with support from the teacher. By 1980, this had shifted in a fundamental way. Schools and teachers are now seen as having the great majority of the responsibility to ensure learning.

This is in the backdrop of factors raising the standards and the stakes for education:

- an exponential increase in the knowledge that exists
- an exponential increase in access to knowledge, both in quantity of knowledge available to the individual and in the speed of access
- an increase in the technical, scientific, and mathematical knowledge base necessary for employment

So far, we have a less natural curriculum, an assembly line process that is less than naturally structured, and a shift in responsibility away from students and their families. Unfortunately, this is not where it stops.

THE PEDAGOGY OF MASS PRODUCTION

As the number of students increase, the expectations on the school increase, and the knowledge base necessary to lead a productive life increases dramatically, what has happened to the pedagogy and organization of the schools? Not much. If you could peer into a classroom in 2008 and a similar classroom in 1958 or even 1908, we know the content has evolved but how different would the teaching techniques be? In the average classroom, very little has changed about how the teacher intends to initiate learning. In the mathematics class, for instance, it is highly likely that you would find the teacher engaging the students in activities that require the rote memorization of facts, practicing procedures for particular symbolic manipulations, and following both with more practice.

The prevalent psychology that undergirds these techniques is called behaviorism, coming out of the work of Skinner (1930's), Gagné (1960's), and the like. Skinner shocked mice with electricity in his experiments about learning. That is certainly not the only animal that has shaped the way we teach. Many of the common methods in today's schools are based to some degree on the work of Pavlov (1890's). You remember Pavlov's dogs, right? Pavlov took hungry dogs and rang a bell each time he would feed them. After doing this enough, he could ring the bell and they would salivate, expecting that food would appear.

Gagné, representing the highest evolution of the implementation of this theory visible in the schools, contributed "Nine Events of Instruction":

1. Gain attention
2. Inform learner of objectives
3. Stimulate recall of prior learning
4. Present stimulus material
5. Provide learner guidance
6. Elicit performance
7. Provide feedback
8. Assess performance
9. Enhance retention transfer

In essence, Gagné was presenting the boiled down version of what all lessons should be like based on this idea of training children to behave in proper ways when confronted with academic questions. If a student is presented with a question (stimulus) "Who was the President of the Confederacy?" the proper response elicited from students through this system would be Jefferson Davis. This psychological model, unfortunately, does not require thinking on the part of the student. All that is required of the student is the response that is taught and rewarded. It also reduces the whole of history to the sum of its facts, much like the assembly line concept assuming that the autos would be of high quality with each person doing the work at their one station. By the 1980s, however, it was commonly believed that American auto makers were producing the poorest quality vehicles in the world. What went wrong with the assembly line? Nobody was asked to think. When they saw something wrong, they did not stop the line.

They merely did their job. Toyota, on the other hand, asked their people to think and work together, seeing the place of their individual role in the context of the entire process. As a result, they continuously received praise for the quality of their vehicles.

When Gagné suggested that we teach all of the parts and then the students would have a whole, he was wrong. U.S. students resemble the autos produced by U.S. manufacturers in the 1970s and 1980s. They are graduating with more knowledge than ever, but with an understanding of it that is less useful than ever. The system broke down

> Our students are graduating with more knowledge than ever, but with an understanding of it that is less useful than ever.

when it was time for the students to hit the road and apply their knowledge. This kind of compartmentalized thinking shows up in the classroom. In mathematics what that looks like is the teacher teaching one section at a time: slope, units, sections, linear equations. In the minds of the students and often the teachers, each chapter is its own entity and once it is done it is gone forever. There is a lack of connection that occurs by the very design. In this system, we build students who can't pull it all together at the end. Beyond this, the lack of connections leads to difficulty in recalling the facts that we have learned. This concept is discussed more in the chapter on how students learn.

IMPACT ON TEACHERS

The limited view of teaching as a collection of stimulus-response pairings extends to teachers as well as students. I love teaching mathematics methods courses. They are focused on the how-to issues of teaching mathematics in a public school. It is my bliss. When I teach a mathematics methods course, my goal is to help the future or current mathematics teacher significantly refine how to think about what mathematics is, how students think about and learn mathematics, and, based on this, how to think about teaching mathematics. The teachers in my methods courses nearly always enter into my course believing they are there to be inactive receivers of a collection of activities. This is based on the idea that the sum of the pieces of knowledge will add up to a whole and practical understanding. Just like in boot camp, we have to break them down before we build them up. They need to reach the conclusion that merely collecting knowledge (math lessons, in this case) is not a good enough goal. They have to be convinced that they do not actually know what they are doing, that mathematics teaching is much more complex than they thought, and that they have a reason to rethink the whole thing. To say it another way, I have to convince them that there is power in the connections within and among mathematics lessons and that the sum of the parts (the collection of lessons they are seeking) is less than the whole (effective mathematics teaching based on a firm understanding of mathematics learning and teaching).

Behaviorist research saw another milestone in the 1980's with the Hunter approach to teaching that has been widely adopted and is still prevalent today in some way, shape, or form:

- objectives
- anticipatory set (hook)
- standards/expectations
- teaching
- guided practice
- independent practice
- closure

Hunter's research was sound. She studied teachers whose students had high achievement scores, the best of the best, to come up with this model containing the elements that most of them shared. The fundamental flaw, however, was that all of them were working on the same assumptions about human learning. If you look at the models carefully, they are based on the same fundamental ideas: if you present things clearly and have the students practice a lot, then you can give them the same stimulus and get them to respond with the correct, desired, and effective response. In short, we are not much better or smarter than the dogs in Pavlov's experiment.

Worse yet, this entire line of reasoning and research just reinforced the educational methods that caused Mark Twain to disrespect formal education publically and repeatedly years before. If this approach to teaching was based on sound research, why have the same mistakes been repeated over and over? It is the same mistake that IBM made about 30 years ago when they scoffed at the idea of a market for personal computers. They had a very profitable business with large computers for business – mainframes. They did research as well: effective research that improved their products. It could have gone on that way for many years, but that is not what happened. The tiny market for the personal computer was not of much interest to them so when the people that developed MS-DOS, the disc operating system for their personal computers, asked for the right to sell the operating system to others, IBM said, "Fine." Oops. In case you missed it, MS stands for Microsoft. Their assumption that the PC market would never be significant caused years of frustration for IBM and helped Microsoft become one of the giants in the industry. Similar to the woes of IBM due to one assumption, students in the U.S. have been suffering from an assumption made by many in educational research: that learning is best thought of in the stimulus and response format. For most of the last century, this was the predominant assumption that informed the honing of educational techniques. Other research agendas were out there, but this one dominated – that is, until recently.

Over the last thirty years, a subset of the educational research community has emerged that is swimming against the current. These researchers have been testing out other assumptions about learning that have little to do with the stimulus-response view of learning. Because of this work, educational research has really come a long way. That being the case, why is the dominant pedagogy still based on the old assumptions of a clear explanation and practice? Like the ways of Anatevka, the sleepy little town in "Fiddler on the Roof," the answer to why things remain much the same is simple: Tradition! Teachers are often victims of their own success. Because they themselves did well enough in the old system, they see no need to differ, regardless of the fact that a great many of their fellow students did not do nearly as well, if they stayed in school at all.

CHAPTER 3:
NATURAL LEARNING

Going back to the comparison, what does natural eating look like? Rather than examining only what we eat, the solution is found in the entire approach to food and eating. Rather than limiting our focus to one aspect of living, healthy eating, we should be thinking about the whole process of healthy living and where healthy eating fits into a healthy lifestyle.

A Fond Memory from Childhood: As I was growing up in Georgia, my father was the symbol of this transitional age of the 20th century. He was born in 1925, raised on a Tennessee farm, became a public school teacher and principal, but his true love was farming. Every afternoon after school and on all the school breaks, he spent his time on the farm, watching the animals, working the garden, or pruning the orchard. There were four of us at home at that time, me, my younger brother, and my father and mother. As boys, we spent time learning how to farm from my father. Each year he planted two sizable gardens and it took all four of us to do the work. Preparing the ground, breaking the ground, and laying out the rows fell to dad and his boys. We would also spend hours weeding, fertilizing, and protecting the plants from bugs and predators. Mom helped plant, pick, and process the food. We learned how to "can" and make preserves from her. In retrospect, it was a tremendous amount of work. It was work that required collaboration, apprenticeship, and achievement. Our parents knew what equipment we could operate, how well we worked and what level of proficiency we achieved. The goal was to turn boys into fully capable men of equal or better quality than their father.

That experience describes life and learning in its most natural state. In the world of fast living and fast food, the process of gathering and preparing the food has been replaced by an hour at the gym and a trip to the grocery store on the way home. It does not have to be that way. We pay big money to wait in line for elaborate machines that simulate the process of pulling weeds (rowing) or repeatedly stomping the shovel into the soil (squats). This is not to mention the fact that you can usually find someone circling the parking lot so they can get a spot close to the door so they do not have to walk too far to go exercise! The food has not been replaced, although we could certainly make better choices. What has been replaced are the natural processes of obtaining food as well as the natural processes involved in preparing it to be consumed, digested, and become a part of us. As a result, we now get less healthy food in a less healthy way.

Like a trip to the gym, we make special attempts to have students exercise (think) on machines (learning activities) that have very little to do with the process that they are simulating. That process is solving real-world problems. In the real world, train A and train B problems do not exist. In the real world, you don't have a need to write a report on an early 18th century English poet. These things just don't happen to 99.999% of us living in our adult lives. Moreover, if these things did occur in our adult lives we may not remember how we handled them in school anyway. Remember Twain's definition?

> "Education is what is left over when you forget everything that your teacher made you memorize when you were in school."

In behaviorism, this phenomenon is referred to as extinction. If you quit rewarding the response, then the response stops occurring. In other words, if you stop practicing and performing for a grade, you are likely to forget whatever it was that you had "learned." To re-harness an old expression: it is NOT just like riding a bike. You do forget!

What, then, is the educational equivalent to healthy learning? Let's talk about riding a bike. It really is the best possible example. Nearly all of us have learned to ride a bike at some point. Nearly all of us believe that even if we have not ridden a bike in 20 years, we could learn to do it again in quick order, if there were any learning to be done at all. It is normal, however, to forget how to do specific mathematics procedures and problems within weeks of learning them. Why is that? What makes the experience of learning to ride a bike so much more powerful than learning to solve Train A and B problems? In other words, what makes a learning process healthy (effective) as opposed to unhealthy (ineffective)?

<u>Bound and Determined</u>: I started to ride a bike much later than everyone else in the world, or at least that is the way it seemed to me. I was (this is embarrassing) eleven years old. Yes, that's right. That's what I said. I was eleven years old. Now, stop laughing! I had a terrible sense of balance, low self-esteem, and my parents were not going to buy me a bike until I could ride one. The same thing happened with my driver's license, but don't get me started. Anyway, back to the bike. I was bound and determined to learn to ride. Everyone was riding circles around me. We were members at a pool over a mile away from our house. My brothers could ride their bikes or even drive over there. I ended up walking or running next to the guys on bikes. It was great exercise, but not the coolest thing in the world.

Here is how the experience went when I finally had unlimited access to a bike. Imagine the scene: A row of houses that are all exactly the same – cracker boxes with no garage. A driveway of about 50 feet from the street to the back of the house, about 20 feet of road and then the neighbors 50 feet of driveway, all open except for a swarm of 5 bikes rolling back and forth. Okay, so five bikes do not qualify for a swarm, but when yours is the only bike not moving, they seem like a swarm. My bike mostly stood still, not moving forward or backwards. No, I kept pushing it upright trying to balance, and then plummeting back to reality! The other kids continued swarming back and forth in an irregular pattern, keeping me dizzy, confused and nervous, as they watched me flounder. I got my courage up one more time, pushed down on the pedal, went about three feet and "SMACK!" right back on the ground. My eyes were watering but real men don't cry, right? I stood back up leaning the bike between my legs and took a deep breath. I pushed down on the pedal for what seemed like the hundredth time (and maybe it was) when the ground started to move beneath me. I was riding!

Starting in the middle of my driveway, I made it most of the way across the street, nearly in the neighbors' drive when I plummeted to the ground triumphantly. Yes, I fell, but so what. I had ridden a bike! It may have only been twenty feet, but I had done it. Instead of jerking violently down to the right or left, I had managed to control that motion enough to stay vertical for at least seven seconds! It was glorious!   After a few more attempts, I even completed a turn without stopping to catch myself. Ever since that day, I have been able to do the basics of bike riding.   Stand, start, glide, balance, turn, and brake without falling.   I was a new man!

Now allow me to point out the critical features of this learning situation that made it successful, as determined by the fact that I can get on any bike in the world at any time and start riding immediately. First, I believed that I had access to the bike.   My brother had given up his old bike.   It was mine to crash as many times as I needed to crash.   There were no consequences to anyone but myself.   Second, at this age, the risks were finally outweighed by the benefits.   The social pressure to ride outweighed my fear of crashing as well as my fear of ridicule.   The ridicule of failure was not nearly as bad as the ridicule of not even trying.   Third, they let me.   By this I mean that nobody was trying to teach me.   I had no adult holding the bike and telling me the same stupid things over and over.   "Keep your balance!"   What a stupid thing to yell at a child!   It is hard to keep something that you never acquired in the first place!

Not every situation is just like that.   In fact, soon thereafter, I taught a couple of my cousins how to ride their bikes.   I wanted to share the joy.   They had the same fears, so how did I manage to help them over those fears?   First, I held the bike seat and the middle of the handle-bars and showed them what balanced and unbalanced felt like.   Sitting on the bike and lifting your feet off the ground is a Wile E. Coyote moment. Sitting on an unbalanced seat is like Wile E. Coyote standing in the middle of the air after he runs straight off the edge of a cliff. He knows he is about to fall to his doom, so he gets that look on his face that we laughed at so many times when I was a kid. Same deal. Nobody wants to fall off of a bike. Lifting your feet off the ground leads to an inevitable "thunk" on the ground. Holding the seat and limiting the amount of fall while still allowing them to feel off balance was the key to success. The risks were then smaller than the benefit. The experience becomes something akin to learning to walk a tightrope. If the worst that could happen is a fall onto a very soft net, it is no big deal. You get the experience without major consequences. It is fun to try. With no net, there is no fun and most people will never give it a real try.

Yet, when given the chance to get on a bike and feel the difference between good balance and bad balance something changes in us. We want to squeeze our legs together and use the muscles in our torso to straighten out. It is just natural. Once my cousins got this idea, it was just a matter of running with them to have them do it while they were moving. After a while, they did it well enough for me to let go and voilà! They are forever bike-riders. Mission accomplished. In a guided and protected fashion they were allowed to experience some failure and scary moments without big consequences. They were empowered to love learning for the sake of learning and, moreover, allowed to focus on the benefits more than the risks. English can be that way. Math can be that way.

What if we had tried it through rote memorization? The bicycle equivalent to the typical mathematics lesson would be to sit them on a stationary bike and have them pedal to their hearts' content and way beyond. Then we would quiz them on stationary bike riding and test them on it. When it came time to go out and actually ride bikes, however, they would simply look at us and say, "You never taught me this." They would be correct. We give students twenty questions to answer about a play they read for English, and then expect them to understand the finer points of theater. Ridiculous! We drill them with flash cards to imprint the facts on their brain and then expect them to know how to solve problems with these facts. No wonder so many of them do random things with the numbers in word problems. We have not put them in true, authentic thinking situations. We have not guided their problem-solving on real issues that they are actually facing.

> No wonder so many of them do random things with the numbers in word problems.

You can't memorize how to ride a bike and expect to be able to do it in real life. It just makes no sense. We do not learn by memorizing first and then practicing. We learn by experiencing, failing, working hard to make adjustments, experiencing success, and honing our skills. Only when real understanding has been reached does it make sense to practice. This, my friends, is the difference between guided natural learning and unnatural learning. It was not accomplished by practicing the right way one hundred times. It was accomplished by getting it wrong one hundred times and working on it until they got it right. I believe this is also referred to in the common vernacular as the school of hard knocks.

WHAT IF

What if we could set up math and science learning situations in which the consistent end result was that the average child would attain and maintain the uncanny ability to approach any mathematics problem with the confidence to know that they can solve it, that it is just a matter of time? Sound brash? Too bold? Too idealistic? Perhaps there might be a bit of Pollyannaistic thinking but there is also a ring of truth. There are teaching techniques that do lead us to believe that mathematicians are not just born but one can become a mathematician, scientist, theologian, or any lofty learning goal through experience! How? It is just like riding a bike.

The critical features of effective teaching are the same as the critical features of learning to ride a bike.

The Situation is Authentic: If the student has no curiosity about the content to be learned, then meaningful and useful learning is unlikely to occur. We are not referring to the motivational aspects, although there are clear benefits. No, the single most important reason to have authentic learning situations is the ideas of transfer and authentic expertise. For over 100 years, scholars have fought over the notion of transfer, the idea that you can learn something in one context and then apply it to a new context. Without going into the details of the debates, it is sufficient to say that transfer is NOT automatic. Context matters. If you break down the tasks of thinking and compartmentalize them as the typical American textbooks do, students will see them as compartmentalized.

In other words, if we work on Shakespeare's material for one unit and Eugene O'Neill's during some other time of the year, there is a good chance that the students will not attempt to take the lessons learned about plays from the Shakespeare lessons and apply them to their thinking about O'Neill's works unless they are prompted to do so. Even then they are challenged in doing so. They may even gripe about how unfair it is to bring up the past (lessons learned 2 months ago). Authentic learning is tackling problems that the *students* see as a problem. Just as in riding a bike, it is possible to guide students into seeing the focus of a lesson as a problem. We are not born into riding bikes; it is a cultural phenomenon. It does not start as something important, but it becomes something important. It becomes an authentic problem to be solved, but how?

<u>Finding Balance Between Risks and Benefits</u>: There are risks involved in learning the English

language that are very similar to learning to ride a bike. There is the embarrassment of mispronouncing or misusing words which can lead to ridicule from those who do it right. There is also the self-deprecation that comes from failure. From the student's perspective, it simply makes no sense to take academic risks if the price outweighs the benefits. In this case, the student needs to understand fully not only the benefit of this instance but the long-term benefit. Riding a bike is a big deal and the benefits are for life. What are the long-term benefits of learning to read poems correctly that are in an ancient English dialect that is long gone from any culture on earth? If we are to have the students be engaged, we must not only work on our classroom environment as a safe place but also examine closely the commonly asked question: "When are we ever going to use this?" The question is much more relevant than most people are comfortable admitting. Without re-examining what and why we teach certain things, we will fail to make significant progress.

Access Includes Staying out of the Way: As Ms. Frizzle so often said on the Scholastic/PBS Kids show The Magic School Bus, "Take chances, make mistakes, and get messy!"[1] Too often the environment in schools is designed to avoid mistakes, as if they were taboo. Children need to know that they can make mistakes without being corrected. Not that mistakes go uncorrected, mind you, but that the children have the opportunity to see the consequences of their mistakes and make the corrections themselves. The three year old that wants to tie her own shoes looks a bit brash when she refuses help from Mom, but at some point it makes sense to allow her to do it for herself. It is not after she knows, but before she knows how to tie her shoes that the letting go process must take place. Giving her the opportunity to make the mistake and trip over her untied shoes gives more meaning to the time when she succeeds. This is closely tied to the other concept of risks and benefits. If you never allow her to risk, you are teaching her that taking risks is dangerous and to be avoided. BAD LESSON! Let go and let them learn.

NATURAL LEARNING IS...

All of this can be summarized in a simple statement: experience is the best teacher. It is experiencing things with one's five senses and trying to make sense out of it that builds and reinforces the paths in the brain. This was confirmed in a report from the National Research Council's Committee on Developments in the Science of Learning that was published in 2000.[2] The processes of making sense of the information gathered through experience causes the building and/or refining of synaptic connections which, in turn, make things easier to remember and use. Those that history has acknowledged as great have all had the benefit of being allowed to experience as much of the world as possible and to make sense out of it. If all learning situations were natural, autonomy would be the goal of every parent, teacher, and mentor that a child ever had. The ability to do things without the help of a parent, teacher, or mentor would be the end goal. In education as in parenting, there would be a lot less "teaching" and a lot more learning. The remainder of the book is dedicated to exploring the idea of natural education and how we might move toward this goal.

> The ability to do things without the help of a parent, teacher, or mentor would be the end goal.

CHAPTER 4:
FROM NATURAL LEARNING
TO NATURAL EDUCATION

What we discussed up to this point is the difference between natural and unnatural learning situations. Before we can go any further, however, we must define the distinction between learning and education. Learning occurs within a person as they process information from experiences, whether they are eating dinner, listening to a radio, watching a toddler play, doing a science experiment, or listening to a teacher lecture. Education, on the other hand, is to purposefully be a catalyst for the learning of specific knowledge, concepts, or practices. Education usually happens with a pre-specified audience of learners (students) and the content is usually a piece of a broader set of learning goals (standards) determined by a committee that does not include the catalyzing agent (teacher). Consequently, in order to explore the salient elements of natural education we must first begin with an understanding of learners and what occurs in them in a natural learning situation. From there, we can begin to understand how to approach the learner to catalyze learning (teach).

All of us that have grown up in the era of ABC's SchoolHouse Rock understand that the human body has a system of electric signals that communicates experiences. We have also been told that the same electrical impulses are bouncing around in our brains. It is said that the brain works something like a computer, just one with a lot of computing power. As computers are evolving now, it is predicted that a common PC will surpass the human brain in its capacity to store and process information. In a poll of technology-savvy people, over 50% believed that this will occur within the next century. One estimate predicts it to happen in the year 2013. Because of studies of the brain and studies in artificial intelligence, we know that it really is a fair comparison to explain learning by examining how a computer works. In a computer, where are facts and the instructions for processes kept? The information is magnetically imprinted onto the hard drive somewhere and the location is cataloged so that it can be retrieved. This is worth repeating. The information is physically located in an electromagnetic way in a specific location. Computers map these things in order to access them; so does the human brain.

THE BRAIN AS A ROAD MAP

If information is stored in particular locations in a brain (hard drive) then thinking is the process of accessing and connecting that information. It is something akin to a road map. If you want to recall and use a fact (visit a city) it is most handy if there is a direct route to that city. Sometimes, however, there is no direct route and we have to go on many different roads to get there. The fewer roads that lead to any particular location, the harder it is for us to get there. Think of learning, then, as the process of construction. To know a fact for the first time, it must be placed on the map. In order to recall a fact, there must be a road going to that particular location. In the brain, these roads are called synaptic connections.[2] Using a fact to solve a problem is equivalent to passing through a town on the way to somewhere else. For each fact then, it makes sense that there are two kinds of things that make that fact (city) more important, useful, and/or easy to use:

- Having more roads that lead in and out of that town
- Broadening the road and making it a faster highway

The brain's equivalent to having more roads (synaptic connections) that lead into a particular town (fact) is to have the student make lots of connections with other facts that they know. We do this not by the stimulus-response lessons of Hunter and Gagné but by activating their old facts and experiences while we construct the new ones. The new fact becomes more of an extension of the old ones rather than just an added dot on the map. The brain's equivalent to broadening the road (connection between facts) and making it a faster highway (quick recall) is to frequently use the connections. It is exactly like when a new trail is blazed through the wilderness. If it is never traveled again, the trail will quickly disappear with the vegetation along the trail filling in over it. If the path is frequented by travelers, it will not become overgrown. In fact, the more superhighways that lead to a particular fact, the quicker it will be to recall and apply that fact. This depiction emphasizes perhaps the most critical fact in academic achievement: it is not practicing a fact in isolation that makes it easy to recall and use, but it is repeatedly using the connections it has to other facts that makes it so. In this same depiction, rote memorization is like placing the same dot on the

> It is not practicing a fact in isolation that makes it easy to recall and use, but it is repeatedly using the connections it has to other facts that makes it so.

map over and over without ever constructing a road that connects it to other important facts.

This understanding of the brain dispels the lie that rote memorization is a good thing. If it is just a fact rather than a pattern then there is no connection and it looks like a "shotgun approach" to learning. If this is a road map then there are a bunch of towns and no way to drive there.

This fits Twain's definition of education; we tend to forget things that we memorize without connections. Memorizing without understanding is like using a helicopter to fly in and establish cities in the middle of a jungle. When you have the helicopter, it is easy to revisit the spot. Once the helicopter has dropped you off back home, it will be incredibly difficult to travel back to the new cities by land. In a jungle with no roads, a trail must be cut through hard labor. If it is not paved the vegetation will soon grown back in and erase the trail. When this occurs in the mind, there is no easy way to get back (recall) and you have a connection that is not going to stay as a connection. The behaviorist model says let's learn this fact a bunch of times by practice. For example, a teacher would say,

> Teacher: "When you see the stimulus of 7x8, your response should always be 56. What is 7x8?"
> Students: "56." [Moaning in synch.]
> Teacher: "Now let's do that fifty more times."

What the teacher is attempting to accomplish is the creation of a superhighway between two towns, known as "7x8" and "56". In learning the multiplication tables, students build many of these pairings. What is the problem with this? First, they were not asked to pave the roads! Paving the road takes a higher level of thinking than rote memorization. That is why behaviorism includes a concept called extinction. Since the road has not been paved, it can become overgrown. If you don't continually travel the path (as with flash cards or constant review), the students are very likely to forget what they once knew very well.

Second, you've not asked the student to develop a path to get to the pairing of 7x8=56. With few or no connections to other knowledge, students find it hard to get to this knowledge if they need to recall it. This is why kids learn their multiplication in third grade and in the next school year they don't remember, in 9th grade they don't remember, and in 12th grade they are still using calculators because it is hard to remember. It is not well connected to other knowledge. While it is important to memorize 7X8=56 and be able to access and use it quickly (automaticity), in the long run it is the connections between these basic fact and other knowledge that aid in retention and recall. This is where knowledge built on the behaviorist model fails. You need to build strong experiences that pave roads to 7X8=56. It needs to be something very basic that they will always have at hand. The idea of a square is something that we use almost every day. Subconsciously we use squares and base decisions on our understanding of them. If you use squares to investigate 7X8 by building a rectangle that is 7 squares long and 8 squares wide, then you have paved a nice road that goes from 7X8 to 56. If you practice and you have built a road based on experience, then you can remember it easily. You have taken care of pairing 7X8=56 and of getting there in the first place by paving it. Things will grow through blacktop if care is not taken, so you do need to revisit this relationship periodically. On the other hand, you don't have to do as much work to revisit this ground compared to the work you would face if you had rotely memorized the fact and left it as a dirt road.

All the locals know that if you're going to Mountain City, TN, there is only one road in and out. If you learn in a way that is hard to get to, then you're going to get what teachers get every year:

"I don't remember."
"We've never done that before."

After a while, teachers often become frustrated with the teachers that worked with their students in the years prior. They are exasperated, wondering, "Why haven't they taught this to the students?" The problem is not a lack of teaching, however. In fact, I have talked to several teachers that have had the experience of teaching students for several years in a row. Their students will make the same claims, telling their teacher that they did not learn what this same teacher has "successfully" taught them last year. Not only were the students taught, but most of them earned C's and above on the content that they seem to lack. The root of the problem is simply the extinction of knowledge learned in a behaviorist, stimulus-response mode.

The paths to knowledge learned in prior months or years are overgrown. That is why students have such difficulty remembering even the basic facts. That is also why chapters 1-4 in the typical textbook are review from the year before. I actually suggest teachers skip chapters 1-4. Students know. It is simply that recalling this information requires hard labor, clearing the overgrown paths. To the teacher that recognizes that students do have this knowledge, the students appear to be lazy-brained. Getting to the facts they are asked to recall is such hard work that they don't want to do it. The students may need to ask themselves questions to relive the experiences that got them there. That is a skill that can be learned. Having four chapters of review each year, however, teaches the student that it is okay to be lazy-brained. They have learned that if they claim to not remember enough times, the teacher is eventually going to reteach it.

Constant reviewing and reteaching in the same stimulus-response mode means that students are basing the same knowledge on a different experience without connecting it to the old one. Students feel like they are starting from scratch in some cases. It creates another weak path. It is more confusing because you don't know which path to take. What happens when you fill a room with objects that are not organized or connected and continue to do that for many years? It makes it hard to move around or find anything. The same kind of clutter that occurs in a room can occur in brains that are filled with scattered bits of unconnected, unorganized knowledge and experiences. This brain clutter occurs because of this approach to teaching and learning.

After years of this, the teenage brainwash occurs - a chemical wash that breaks chemical connections in the brain. According to Dr. Jay Giedd of the National Institute of Mental Health, in the mid-teens, teenagers lose connections to a process called pruning in which the brain is restructuring.[3] This is why parents think their child is changing in drastic ways and often feel as if they don't know them anymore. In an interview with PBS's Frontline, Dr. Geidd stated that, "Those cells and connections that are used will survive and flourish. Those cells and connections that are not used will wither and die." In other words, the brain is prioritizing and getting rid of extra connections. When your child reaches the age of 25, you suddenly become a genius to your child. It is because of the brainwash. If you don't make each important path to knowledge a paved and well traveled road, then it will be washed out.

The image of learning as road construction and use also dispels the notion that many teachers believe about the "dangers" of teaching more than one way to solve a problem. I have often heard teachers say that they will avoid discussing multiple solutions "because it will just confuse the students." This may be so, but only because many students only know how to deal with facts (cities) and know precious little about how to connect and use those facts (roads).

CONNECTIONS AND EXPERTISE

We are fascinated by those people who are known for making connections. Books, movies and shows about great detectives like Sherlock Holmes and crime scene experts continue to be top-rated. It is not just the joy of seeing the good guys win over the bad guys. We all experience a sense of adventure in making connections and take joy in the process of trying to make conjectures and solve the crime as we discover the evidence with the characters. It is precisely how one sees facts as connected that make one an expert or a novice in any field.

In his book about Communities of Practice,[4] Wenger describes the culture of insurance claims processors and the process that they go through when they learn to work in that environment. He paid particular attention to how they moved from being a novice to becoming an expert. What they taught people was not just pieces of knowledge but how to solve problems that are new. How do they go about processing a claim that doesn't fit into a neat category? It is a process that they go through. There are forms and various ways of reporting on the forms that feed the process. It requires some level of adaptive expertise, the ability to adapt old information and processes to deal with a new problem that requires new knowledge (towns) and/or new connections (roads). Beyond this new knowledge (add-ons to the map), the learner also has to access bits of information AND be able to communicate them to others.

Whoever has solved the most new problems has the highest level of expertise and therefore rank. This is how a group of people rises to the level of a profession. As Flexner pointed out in 1915 in his report investigating the medical profession, a profession has four major attributes.[5] The one everyone recognizes immediately is knowledge beyond the layperson. The expertise of doctors and lawyers is commonly understood, yet there are three more attributes. One of them is collegiality. The knowledge base gets extended through collegiality which keeps it above the layperson. Even with WebMD and all the books available, we still recognize doctors as necessary. The third part is altruism. It is the fact that they are not just in it for themselves. We expect doctors to have our best interest in mind and we are angry if we find out otherwise. Those doctors make the news and often go to prison. Unlike the common depiction, lawyers want to help too. The last attribute is autonomy. The idea that doctors monitor doctors, the AMA and medical boards in each state. Lawyers police the lawyers (e.g. Duke Lacrosse rape case). Those are the attributes we are looking at on the individual and collective level.

If we want our students to act like professionals when they enter the work force, we must provide an education that encourages professional behavior. When you enter insurance claims, you are expected to build your knowledge base to a certain point not known by the average person. In every job, you're supposed to have other people's best interest in mind and work together to extend the knowledge base, getting better at what you do. Every boss should be able to expect that their workers can be given an assignment, whether individual or collective, which an employee or employees can accomplish without the boss's help. Given a question or assignment, an employee should be able to return to the boss with a firm answer and explain why it is right. That process is a basic expectation of employers. What employers have been saying for quite some time, however, is that their young employees don't know how to solve new problems. Employers also commonly complain that younger employees do not know how to collaborate to solve problems. The bottom line is that regardless of how well intentioned the people in our education system may be, the processes that are healthy and natural for learning are not among the things that the system is encouraging.

EDUCATION AND THE ADVENTURE OF HEALTHY LEARNING!

To reiterate, strong learning consists not of learning distinct facts in a rote manner, but in the learner having numerous experiences traveling to and from that fact multiple times and in as many ways as reasonably possible. If this is the case for learning, what implications does this have for education? In other words, how do we create, structure, and facilitate experiences that are most likely to lead to strong natural learning? The short answer: We need a shift from delivery to inquiry. The long answer: We need to send students on adventures regularly.

Going back to the food analogy, in the stimulus-response, lecture/rote mode of instruction, there is no hunting, no growing, no cooking and therefore, no power. It may lead to immediate gratification (good quiz scores) but empty calories lead to being hungry soon. Healthy minds hunt and grow. That means having hunger and going about addressing that hunger in the most basic and appropriate ways. In terms of education, this means having questions to answer, doing the work to have enough information, and engaging in the process of applying that information in new and old ways to reach a solution. In the language of education, this process can be described as synthesis and metacognition. In the language of maps, it is rearranging your cities and roads until it all makes sense in light of the old experiences as well as the new experiences. Eating healthy means you worked for it. It is not canned food or fast food. That means you will have the ability to transfer that knowledge into new environments. What kind of experiences lead to this kind of learning? Challenging ones.

Simulated Adventures: I had taken video games away from Jake and Madison, the worst possible punishment that a parent could do. Karen, my wife, said, "You're dooming our children to failure." I was thinking, "What? Are you nuts? We're talking about video games!" Unfortunately, it makes sense if you think about it. The way we live in America today, video games represent the most meaningful adventure and problem solving experiences in which they engage.

> Over one billion dollars of research goes into finding out what kids want to do with their time and money.

Kids know that they are supposed to be adventurers: a knight, a damsel in distress. They are supposed to be heroes, described well by John Eldridge in "Wild at Heart." If they don't have an adventure they will find one. If they don't have a positive one, they'll find a negative one. They will be doomed to failure. The gaming and phone industries know this all too well. Over one billion dollars of research goes into finding out what kids want to do with their time and money. The answer: Challenging adventures! Since this research is done by technology based industries, our children spend hours every day trying to "beat the game," whether they are at home, in the car, or even in class at school (where the electronic toys are strictly forbidden).

Many students handle education as "beating the teacher" just like "beating the monster" at the end of the level of the video game. You have to figure out what the monster is going to do, you have to figure out what is going to have an impact on the monster, and you have to do it before the monster does something bad to you. A lot of our straight A students are literally working their tails off to get a grade and could care less whether they learn or not! This explains why the top notch students are the most likely to cheat: If the goal is the grade, and the process of engaging and learning (time consuming, energy consuming) takes away from their ability to score high in all seven classes then they have got to find alternative ways to beat the teacher.

Natural education is an adventure. Some teachers get that. Most of them don't because they came up in the same system. The common perception of the life of university professors is that they sit in their office, study, and teach. They can't imagine something more boring. My experience as a college professor has led me to see being a professor at a major research university as a constant adventure. There is a constant discussion among the probationary faculty at our department, the pull between their natural bent towards inquiry and their natural bent toward service to the schools, versus the university's heavy-handed requirement that they publish in top-notch research journals in large quantities. The reality of the situation is that not only are you supposed to go on an adventure and serve people and learn a bunch, but it is literally our job to periodically share what we've learned so that other people can go on a similar journey with that knowledge. Rather than being a burden it is sharing the message. This is parallel to the knights telling the story of slaying the dragon when they return to the castle. This storytelling about our great learning adventures is crucial. The reason we must tell stories, other than self-aggrandizement, is to motivate the squires (students) to become knights (active learners).

EDUCATION AS DRAGON-SLAYING

What are the basic aspects that comprise a learning adventure? A problem to solve (dragon), a reason to solve it (damsel in distress), and the resources to make it happen (horse, armor, squire). What does this look like in the life of an average adult? The boss says, "We need to make a decision about something." Your job is then to gather a team, collect as much information as you can about the various options, benefits, deficiencies, develop a decision making tool, and prepare to present an argument for the solution that you picked. Not only do you have to hunt, grow, and cook but you're feeding the boss and you have to do it as a team (chef, kitchen). You've got a full-blown adventure, all the makings of a very natural and healthy learning experience, and a reason to develop and employ your adaptive expertise.

When students first run into this kind of learning situation, they often freak out. After experiencing many years of the behaviorist, monkey-see/monkey-do approach where they've been given lectures and worksheets, students are often paralyzed by a natural learning environment. They are not used to making or revisiting connections. They are not used to coming up with ideas on their own. They have spent years looking at the textbooks to tell them what to do. They look for those box-worthy snippets of knowledge. The important piece of knowledge is in a box, usually in a bold color, to draw the student's attention. Students will ignore the rest of the material because they know the box is the only important idea. In a healthy learning adventure, however, you leave the box empty and let the student figure out what idea should be in the box. It is saying, "Here is the knowledge that you learned up to this point, take it and use it in a completely different problem." The process becomes the focus of the lesson rather than the product. You want both, but as long as you focus on the product, students ignore process and then we become frustrated with them when they don't think.

When this approach is taken in the social sciences, the measureable outcome is represented in something called a research paper. When my daughter was asked to write her first research paper on the topic of Thanksgiving, she really did not understand it at all. It was frustrating for her because she was not used to forming her own questions to answer, answering them, and then asking more questions. She thought that "the answer must be in the book somewhere." It had always worked that way before. What would lead her to believe that it might be different in this assignment? She continually pestered me to help her know what to copy out of the book. Furthermore, she believed that she should have the same exact wording as in the book for any idea. Otherwise she could not possibly get it right! The idea of higher level thinking rarely occurs in the K-12 experience of many students. The opportunities are presented, but if the student waits or plays helpless long enough, the teacher will usually bail them out.

The same goes for the teachers that have entered my courses. It is normal for high school math teachers to look at any new problem and generate an equation. They want to use equations to solve every problem. That's great, but it is only one way to solve the problem. Often someone with fewer mathematics courses can solve a problem in a much more efficient way without ever going to an equation. Both of them use patterns and the equation will always work, but as Dr. Mangho Ahuja used to say in our AP Calculus workshops, "Never use a sledge hammer where a ball-peen hammer will do." One example of what he meant is that you can quickly find the vertex of a parabola by using $x=-b/(2a)$, an Algebra 1 solution strategy, without taking the derivative of its equation, a Calculus 1 solution strategy. It is all about knowing patterns and being able to analyze things efficiently.

As a college professor, I have engaged in my own adventures in figuring out the most effective ways to engage students and have them be effective. Darris and I independently came to similar conclusions about what ought to be major goals in our teaching even though the content we teach, Biblical Greek and mathematics education, is vastly different. In both disciplines, people commonly think of learning as a process of rote memorization. Darris learned by observing student behavior as a fellow student, in recalling his own reactions and responses as a student, and in comparing those with his contemporaries. Then he began to apply those observations and collect others as a teacher which further refined his approach. Darris took what he knew of the individual class as well as what he knew the general life situation of the students to be.

I, on the other hand, taught mathematics in the public schools for five years before beginning formal study of mathematics education at a university. After five years of doctoral work and seven years in the role of professor at a major university, I have learned through the trial and error followed by much more rigorous studies. It was just a few years ago when I finally understood the most basic idea: students are always trying to learn. All we have to do is give them the right tools, set them in the right direction, and insist that they think thing s through. Done this way, learning ceases to be passive and transforms into the adventure that it education should be.

The students often don't initially understand the point of this kind of teaching, but when they do adjust, more students learn and more students remember it. More importantly, they can apply their newly acquired knowledge well beyond their time in the course. It is worth repeating Mark Twain's comment one more time: "Education is what is left when you forget everything that the teacher made you memorize."

CHAPTER 5:
NATURAL EDUCATION
FOR STUDENTS

If natural learning is complex, natural education is even more so. There was an argument in a major research journal, where someone was arguing against constructivism—the idea that students build their own knowledge. One of the arguments was that it took mathematicians thousands of years to build up the knowledge base through calculus that represents the K-12 knowledge base. The response to the "thousands of years" argument was that the reason it took thousands of years is that the situation has to be right to stimulate thinking to those conclusions. Teachers can simulate conditions that trigger the need to come to those conclusions in a way that bypasses a hundred years of experience. This chapter is about what those experiences look like. What do the students go through when they are doing it?

I used to think that only mathematics teachers had the answer to this figured out. The National Council of Teachers of Mathematics, comprised of around 100,000 mathematics teachers from elementary schools, middle schools, high schools, colleges, and other professional organizations as well, produced a document of monumental significance in 1989 and a revised version in 2000. These documents outlined what mathematics is important in K-12. Beyond this, however, it added for the first time, specific standards for mathematical processes. Given equal weight with algebra, geometry, measurement, statistics, and number, were problem solving, communication, representation, reasoning/proof, and connections. That is right, *connections*. These are the same connections that we spoke of earlier in our description of the brain in the learning process. Moreover, the representation standard outlined the idea that there should be many paths to understand an idea, many roads in to the same knowledge.

I was proud that mathematics had this figured out until the day I went to the meeting to develop curriculum for the Tennessee Governor's Academy for Mathematics and Science. Lo and behold, I had the opportunity to peruse the standards in several other content areas and, guess what? They had process standards, too! All of them had similar notions:

- that students should explore ideas, tools, and relationships in order to build an understanding
- that the students should experience knowledge in many different forms and from different perspectives

In other words, all of the areas had figured out that a useful and important concept or skill (city) should have many ways to access/apply it (roads) that are created and paved through experience. I was both humbled and elated. Most of us call the student-oriented process of constructing cities and roads the same thing: inquiry. That's right, inquiry: the simple task of asking questions, answering them, and analyzing the strength of our process and solution.

LEARNING VIA TOOLS OF INQUIRY

(ADVENTURES WITH PLAY-DOH)

There are many different approaches to natural learning through making sense of experiences. One such approach is the classic and very popular Five E Model from science: "Engage, explore, explain, expand, and evaluate". In mathematics, there are very few important concepts that cannot be studied and learned in this matter. One of my favorite activities involves Play-doh and rice and comes from an awesome curriculum called <u>Connected</u>

<u>Mathematics</u>.[6] The lesson follows after another lesson in which the students have learned and practiced the ideas of the volume of a cylinder, including the formula and why it is what it is. In this Play-doh activity, they form a sphere, make a cylinder of the same height, and then squish the Play-doh sphere into the cylinder. It turns out that the volume of the sphere is 2/3 of the volume of the cylinder.  After removing the Play-doh, a cone is constructed to have the same base and height which are the same as the cylinder. Using the cone and dry rice as a measuring device, they discover that the volume of the cone is 1/3 of the volume of the cylinder. With a little symbolic manipulation and substitution, the students reach the conclusion that the formula for the volume of a sphere is $\frac{4}{3}\pi r^3$ and that the formula for the volume of a cone is $\frac{1}{3}\pi r^2 h$. Not only are middle grade students capable of reaching these conclusions without being told, but they remember them for a long time because they made connections. They made an emotional connection with childhood experiences of squishing Play-doh, but they also made mathematical connections between different but related shapes and their volume formulas.

In the above example, multiple representations of the volume of solids are used. Play-doh, rice, drawings, and equations all end up being used to describe the volume of a sphere and analyze its relationship to that of a cylinder and a cone. The use of multiple representations is the road map equivalent of creating or activating a lot of roads to the same town. You can think of frequent problem solving as having students develop a GPS system or MapQuest-like tool for their thinking processes. Solving problems makes them travel the connections (roads) they have constructed to get to the knowledge (cities) they need to access in order to solve the problems.

Before you assume that we are presenting attention to the processes of problem-solving and learning multiple representations of the same content as the simple approach that will be the answer to all of the education woes in America, let me point out its place in the process of education. This next section puts the aforementioned approach, inquiry, into perspective and weaves the story of the complexity of learning and, hence, education.

The analysis of bike riding in chapter 3 was somewhat informal, sort of off-the-cuff rambling about what might make bike-riding a more natural experience than the typical lesson in school. In order to examine it from a more structured viewpoint, we need a framework. A framework sets the boundaries for thinking by defining broad categories of issues to be considered, thereby offering a tool that can guide our thinking as we analyze the experience. A framework for learning is under development as of March 2008 by researchers in mathematics education.[7] Regardless of how you think learning occurs, your learning theory, this framework is helpful in identifying all of the salient attributes of a learning experience.

In its simplest form, the framework consists of three basic questions:

- What are they to learn?
- How are they to learn it?
- In what context are they to learn it?

While these three questions seem very simple, there are a lot of complexities rolled into each one. Moreover, the interaction between questions makes it an incredibly complex system for analyzing learning.

In my experience of learning to ride a bike, what was to be learned consisted of bike riding. It may sound simple enough, but you have to consider that it includes the critical notions of balance, inertia, centripetal force, and controlling one's balance through the tightening and loosening of muscles in the torso, just to name a few aspects. Not only that, but you have to consider the pedagogy of bike riding. That is to say that you have to consider how people usually learn to ride, what mistakes they usually make, and how they learn to overcome those mistakes and become proficient riders.

The next question of how they are to learn it consists of more not-so-easy notions such as how people begin to explore bike riding in a natural way, how different people might approach solving the problem differently, and how people analyze their mistakes in an effort to learn from those mistakes. Yes, this is brain surgery. People are trying to realign their thinking to match reality. This is a kind of self-service brain surgery referred to as metacognition, thinking about one's own thinking in an effort to improve it. Also rolled into the question of how they are to learn it is the set of beliefs that they take into the situation. If you are trying to teach someone that has decided that they will never be able to balance on a bike, the learning situation is vastly different than with someone who has reached the conclusion that they are really close to knowing it. It greatly impacts how they will learn and, therefore, how you must teach. Their work ethic also greatly impacts how they are to learn. If they tend to avoid hard work, they are very unlikely to stick with the experience of picking up the bike 100 times before learning.

As for the third question, it takes little convincing for most folks to believe that context matters. Some will only approach the bike if nobody is looking. The audience matters. Some will only find it a worthwhile endeavor if their friends are there to encourage them. The relationship with the teacher matters as well. If they have a bossy, negative teacher forcing them to learn how to ride a bike, it will be a very different learning experience than if they have someone that is supportive and sensitive to their emotional needs. Such a teacher is much more likely to find the right approach to speed up the learning process. Another aspect of the environment is the catalysts. If there is a bike-a-thon coming up with the church youth group, a person formerly resigned to a life without biking may be suddenly highly motivated.

A LEARNING FRAMEWORK

While this was a slightly more structured look, it does not account for everything in everyone's experience of learning to ride a bike. Expanding on our three questions will allow us to get into further details of what to consider when designing and evaluating an educational experience. For years, teachers have denied the power of educational research. They frequently claimed that it was not practical, that it did not recognize the challenges of their particular students, their particular school district, and/or the way that their students like to learn. The framework is presented here as a way for teachers and those supporting their work to consider all of the major issues involved in a learning experience. It empowers them to consider enough aspects to solve the problem of "How can I use the results of research in my setting?" It identifies three basic and inarguable assumptions.

The first assumption is that content is never as simple and straightforward as it seems. There are distinctive ways that people learn specific content as well as numerous new and interesting ways to get it wrong. Each particular topic or learning goal (e.g. recognizing an improper use of the present participle in 7th grade English) may have a unique approach that is especially effective. An elementary teacher may have as many as 7 major learning goals each day of the school year. A middle grades teacher may have as few as 2 or 3 goals if they teach the same grade level or class each day. Still, with 180 school days, that leaves a lot to learn if we are going to teach effectively.

Assumptions Made for the Framework for Natural Learning

1) Content is never as simple & straightforward as it seems.
2) We all ask questions constantly and seek to answer them.
3) Different students will be thinking completely differently about the same thing on a regular basis.

The second assumption is that we all ask questions constantly and seek to answer them. This bears repeating: we are all in a constant state of inquiry. Before you go throwing stones and complaining about lazy students that do not want to answer questions, I should point out that I did not say that the questions that students ask are well-aligned with the questions we want them to be asking. From my own experience, I know of several students whose main question was, "How do I get Mr. Taylor to shut up and let me sleep?" There are many other questions in a similar vein that students ask. Even the highest achieving students may be asking something like, "How do I get Mr. Taylor to give me an A with the least amount of effort?" The trick, of course, is to find ways to get them to engage in inquiry on the questions that we have designed into our lessons, the questions that lead to learning the particular content which is the goal for the day.

The third and final assumption is that different students will be thinking completely differently about the same thing on a regular basis. Their beliefs about history will color how they view any assignment. Their need to rebel against all authorities, which may stem from their experiences ten years ago, will impact whether they will accept the questions that are posed. Some students are more easily enticed into engaging the content by sports references and many others will shut down at any reference to anything resembling competition. In short, people are complicated. Since assembly-line education requires connecting with as many as 35 students at a time, this really is one of the most challenging careers on the face of the planet. Examine what this means at the middle or high school level. Meeting the challenge of engaging 35 students in the learning of one or two particular and technical pieces of content means engaging 35 different sets of experiences, 35 levels of understanding of the content, and 35 unique sets of beliefs. Many teachers take on that daunting task with 6 classes each day (6 x35= 210) for 180 days a year. Teaching is hard.

With these assumptions in mind, let's look at the full framework, an expanded version of the three questions. Before we do, however, I should add a caveat. This framework is one that is being worked on by a great many people.[7] I claim neither originality nor ownership. I only claim that the framework is real and practical. It is important to consider all aspects of the framework to obtain a full view of any educational situation. In fact, it is my claim that natural education begins when you have considered all aspects and aligned the experience in ways that encourage the students to see your intended questions as their questions. In the absolute best student learning experiences, all six stars in this system align. Those are the moments that move teachers to tears, when they remember why they entered this low-paying, low-status, thankless job in the first place. Light bulb moments arise from proper use of this framework. You know those moments, when the struggling student gets really big eyes stares at the teacher, drops their jaw, and exclaims, "I get it!"

It is important to remember that this was designed to be a framework for examining what the teacher needs to know and think through when thinking about student learning. Now that we have got your attention and your curiosity is aimed to the framework, here it is:

What are they to Learn?

Content

* What is the nature of what they are going to learn?
* What processes occur when studying this content?

Pedagogy

* How do people learn this content?
* How should you approach teaching this content?
* What mistakes do learners usually make with this content and how should they be guided through and beyond these mistakes?

How are they to learn it?

Curiosity

* What gets people to engage in exploring this content?
* How do people naturally approach the problem?
* What are some key ways to get them to evaluate and think about their thinking?

Orientation

* What do the learners believe about the content to be learned?
* What do the learners believe about their ability to master the content?
* What habits, patterns, and ethics are learners bringing to the learning situation?

In what context are they to learn it?

People

* What is the relationship between the teacher and the learners?
* Are there diverse learners to be taught simultaneously?
* Why are they in this learning situation?
* Are learners' goals aligned with the teacher's goals?

Environment

* Is this environment more conducive to collaboration or competition?
* Who is the leader in the situation and what are they doing that helps or hinders the learning?
* What catalysts have led to this learning situation?

As complex as it is, natural education is:

- Problem solving when the students believe that there is a problem to solve
- The process of apprenticeship, where the teacher guides the problem solving process with an eye to meeting the standards of the customer (the world beyond school)
- An identifiable process of moving from the novice stage, being led towards being an autonomous expert, leading others through the understanding and use of the content to be learned

In natural education, the teacher's goal with regards to any content is to have the students no longer need to be taught, even in the face of new content.

A CAUTIONARY WORD

As a result of the intricacies of natural learning, it is neither possible nor desirable to create a one-size-fits-all curriculum that could be packaged for delivery to the masses. To do so would be to go back to the mass production model which is unnatural and, in many cases, ineffective. That is not to say that there are not excellent curricula available. I already cited one that I think is very compatible with natural learning. What it means is that the teacher plays an incredibly crucial role in how such a curriculum plays out in the classroom with the particular students, in the particular setting. This makes teacher education both incredibly crucial and incredibly challenging.

CHAPTER 6:
NATURAL LEARNING & NATURAL
EDUCATION FOR TEACHERS

If students are to be held to the standard of thinking their way through things, having questions, and going to answer them, then teachers ought to be held to this standard as well. Any teacher that does not think of themselves as a learner should be fired. I mean it. What their students learn from them is that the content is dead, that there is no adventure, and that school is something that you survive. It is difficult to teach learning as an adventure if you do not live that way. For several years now, I have taught a course for doctoral students entitled *Research Trends in Mathematics Teacher Education.*

The practical mantra that I repeat constantly throughout the semester is this:

Whatever is good for students is also good for teachers.

For you mathematics folks, I like to call it the Fundamental Theorem of Mathematics Teacher Education. The most fundamental concept that I want my doctoral students, who are teacher educators, to learn in this course is that teachers need to inquire about student inquiry. In other words, teachers need to go on adventures for their own learning as they focus on supporting the natural learning of their students. This is not the same as requiring teachers to engage in continuing education or to earn a master's degree. While these formal settings sometimes allow for natural learning, they are most frequently driven by the questions of the instructor rather than being driven by the teachers who are the learners in these settings.

The teacher needs to know how to learn in a natural way and support students' learning in a natural way. In order to do this, the teacher needs to know both the content and the curriculum inside and out. Successfully completing a college degree in history, science, English, or mathematics does not mean that a person knows the content of middle school or high school inside and out in that subject. In fact, it often serves to give them a false sense of confidence about how well they understand the content. Even if they do know the content that well, content is only one sixth of the framework. If teachers are not well-versed in all six aspects of natural learning, then they are unlikely to be able to support natural learning for students.

Most people, however, enter the field of teaching because they want to share their knowledge base and because of the love that they have for the content. Convincing them that they actually know very little of what they need to know to teach effectively is a daunting task. That makes teacher education one of the most complex and frustrating endeavors in which one could engage. Each future teacher must be convinced that despite their thirteen years in the public schools and four years of college they actually know very little of what there is to know about teaching and learning. It is not that those experiences and successes are tossed aside. A good teacher educator will use their knowledge and experiences as connection points from which to launch an investigation, asking future teachers to make sense out of those old experiences in light of their new understanding of teaching and learning. This is natural teacher education: revisiting old connections while paving new roads to add to their thinking and knowledge base.

Moreover, since natural learning is different than what most teachers have experienced in their own education, then teachers need to come to understand the truth of Twain's definition of education. They need to understand that the behaviorist task analysis format curriculum is unnatural and ineffective. Teachers need to experience enough of the limitations of unnatural education to be asking questions about how to teach in a way that encourages natural learning. Teachers need to experience natural education from a students' perspective and then learn how to facilitate episodes of natural learning with their own students. In case you missed it, there were three parts to the process we described:

- Awareness that the unnatural way does not work
- Experience as a student in the natural way
- Learning how to facilitate natural learning

This was just as true in my own experience. Do you remember the story of Sally and her impact on my own development as a teacher and teacher educator? I had been growing less and less comfortable with the way I was teaching but I did not know how to access anything else. I then had the opportunity to attend some workshops where the presenters took the participants, high school teachers, through well-written textbooks that supported natural learning. They did not lead us through as teachers, however; we actually went through a unit as if we were students. This allowed us to re-develop our viewpoint from the student perspective. We periodically reflected on that from the teacher perspective, discussing what we thought our students would do and how to avoid potential pitfalls. When I got back to the classroom, however, I still did not really know how to change my everyday teaching. The lab activity where Sally and her classmates bounced balls and graphed data was the best I had to offer. Unfortunately, it was the only natural learning that occurred that year for Sally. This is why I took it so hard. I knew that there was a better way to do it but I did not know how to implement this new way.

Unfortunately, this is all too common. As outlined in The Teaching Gap[8], teachers that know there is a better way to teach often do not know how to accomplish it. They either make failed attempts at natural education or, just like students, refuse to try because they have not been shown how to do every lesson that way. If they have no image

> In order to teach effectively, teachers must literally know their content backwards and forwards.

to replace the old one, a well-informed teacher is still likely to default to the unnatural education. Why? The answer is simple. In order to teach effectively, teachers must literally know their content backwards and forwards. They must not just be able to lead and explain but must also be able to reverse-engineer student's wrong thinking to figure out where they may have gone wrong.

When teachers experience episodes of natural learning, they are investigating mathematical patterns and figuring out why things are the way they are. What they learn is that the processes that they go through as a teacher can be done by a student with powerful results. Just as teachers should be engaged in looking for patterns of correct and incorrect thinking, students should be checking their thinking as well as the thinking of others. All teachers probably agree to the old adage that says that you learn more about something when you have to teach it. This simple saying recognizes the power of being challenged with questions, exploring something backwards and forwards, in all the ways there are to know it. Natural learning for students is about the students teaching themselves and becoming their own authority with their own measure of expertise. When the teacher understands that, they begin to see the power.

Teachers need to experience making significant connections from the student perspective because they may not know what it is like. They may not know what it is like to be an efficient learner as opposed to an efficient student who is trying to beat the teacher. It is the difference between cleaning because you have to, meaning you'll do as little as possible, and cleaning because it is important to be clean. Teachers need to experience what it is like to have a full learning experience and value it for its achievement. Once the teacher experiences that, then and only then will they be able to effectively analyze those processes and figure out how they can support those processes. Another way to describe the process is re-learning how to learn.

NATURAL EDUCATION FOR TEACHERS

What does it look like, when we are purposing to give a teacher these kinds of experiences? As a teacher educator, what does natural education of future and/or current teachers look like? Short answer: Same process, different content. Let's examine some successful experiences through the learning framework outlined in chapter 5. As we discuss these experiences, we will highlight some of the things that are unique to teacher education, which require the teacher educator to pay attention to their own learning process while they pay attention to the teacher's learning process while the teacher pays attention to K-12 students' learning processes as well as their own. (Revisit the diagram on page seven if I lost you on that one. ☺)

TED SLAYS LINEAR INEQUALITIES

Ted was a second-career guy. He had made some money and now he was coming to the university to become a middle grades mathematics teacher and make a difference. He was a student teacher at a local middle school while he took my mathematics methods course. That semester, I had decided to require that all of the students engage in lesson studies. Imported from Japan as a way for teachers to learn while they improved the curriculum, lesson study had been a hot topic at the research conferences. I had tried it out with current teachers at a rural school and with my secondary mathematics methods course the previous year, so I knew just how effective it could be. The American version of lesson study takes many forms and it is easily Google-able, so I will describe what it looks like in the Taylor-ized form ☺.

Step 1) Choose a team of at least three teachers. The student teachers usually choose a team of three student teachers. Once in a while, one of their mentors or another licensed teacher will work with the interns.

In Ted's case, the other two members of his team were his mentor teacher and another teacher at that school. These veteran teachers were intrigued by the idea of lesson study and, modeling good behavior for their students, they wanted to learn.

Step 2) Choose a mathematics topic from one lesson. The topic MUST fit into the regular teaching schedule of all teachers on the lesson study team. This usually takes the form of one lesson selected from the regular schedule.

Ted asked his mentoring teacher, "What topic do 7th grade students struggle with the most?" Without hesitation and with agreement from a nearby colleague, his mentoring teacher said, "linear inequalities." Have you ever noticed that the word "question" begins with "quest"? Through this question, Ted, his mentoring teacher, and a colleague were all activated: commissioned to go on a quest to conquer the dragon (linear inequalities) that had slain so many seventh graders.

For those of you who may have forgotten, inequalities include "greater than" or "less then" symbols in addition to or in place of the equals sign such as in 2x-4<3.

Step 3)   Read peer-reviewed journal articles and research articles to learn about:

- What are some curriculum topics with which it is naturally connected
- How students learn the topic
- What difficulties they commonly have
- How teachers have successfully helped the students overcome those difficulties
- How to assess the learning of that particular topic; what ideas/skills should be the focus of the assessment and which problems or types of assessments most effectively bring out the students' understanding

Ted had a lot of trouble finding research that was specific to linear inequalities, especially at a seventh grade level. He did, however, manage to find some related topics that ended up being crucial in determining the outcome of this adventure.

Step 4)   Develop a lesson plan, or refine an old one, that employs all of the major lessons learned from reading those peer-reviewed articles.   My students are required to justify every part of these lessons from the articles.

Step 5)   One member of the team teaches the lesson to the student while the other members observe. The observers pay close attention to what the students are doing, what they might be thinking, and why they might be thinking that. Data is collected that reflects that student thinking and a debriefing meeting is held to understand why the teacher made the decisions that they did during the lesson.

Step 6)   Based on the data collected, the lesson is refined. Any refinement MUST be based on student data such as quizzes, writing assignments, questions that they asked in class, or any other student generated information.

Step7)   Another member of the team teaches the revised lesson in their classroom. After a debriefing and analysis meeting, the lesson is again refined based on student generated data.

Step8)   The third member of the team teaches the revised lesson in their classroom. After a debriefing and analysis meeting, the lesson is again refined based on student generated data.

If this were on television, it might be called CSI: Classroom Response Unit. We must be able to convict the students of learning the content based on evidence. Any notions about teaching and learning this lesson that are not based on evidence must be thrown out. They are inadmissible in a court of natural education. After going through this rigorous process with ongoing input from the professor, Ted was stoked! "I have learned so much from this lesson study!"

Ted and his team of experienced teachers learned together that even though the different parts of the lesson appeared to be able to be done in any order, they found that there was an order that worked better. Everything they learned is explainable through the visualization of building roads (connections) to the town (Linear Inequality-ville). The order of events they did makes sense because of where the town is located on the kid's brain map. Meanwhile, the teachers knew the mathematics better than most people after the experience. Those three know how to learn to teach mathematics better than most teachers. That is the magic of teacher inquiry.

JACKIE SLAYS HER PRECONCEIVED NOTIONS

Jackie entered my methods class in the fall with a firm expectation to teach the way she'd been taught. She expected to walk into the classroom, put examples on the board, and make them practice. Jackie was very much opposed to the idea that it was more complicated than this and argued passionately against this "new" approach in the first several class periods in my methods course. As with so many secondary teachers, she had done well in the old system and enjoyed it. Jackie wanted to share that joy with her students. This truly is a great motivation for many teachers and how can we argue against sharing joy, right?

Also like many secondary teachers she was not just there to share *how* she had learned but Jackie was there to teach *what* she loved to learn, Algebra II and above. When I was presenting the importance of using technology, she would say that calculators are evil because the student doesn't have to do the math. This is a misguided viewpoint based on an inappropriate view of mathematics, or any content for that matter. If mathematics is a collection of procedures, then we would not need to teach it in the schools. The calculators and computers would do it all and we would not need to know. On the contrary, mathematics is about the concepts. The procedures are merely tools to help us apply the concepts. In a natural mathematics education, the student does conceptual things, which is the essence of mathematics, and the student uses technology to quickly do the procedures.

The joy in the mathematics, you see, stems from the processes and their interactions with the content, not from the procedures. In her student teaching, Jackie ended up teaching the lowest level students the content that she had not come to teach. Being in the program before I instituted lesson study as the required research mode, Jackie's chosen research project was using technology to reach lower level students. Why would she choose this when she argued against technology? She wanted to know why research seemed to support the use of technology. She was taking the challenge head-on. It had become her quest.

Jackie read an incredible amount of research, and followed it as closely as possible given her context. She utilized dynamic geometry software to teach focusing on the concepts first and procedures second for a whole 4-week unit. She came away from the experience with several revised beliefs:

- Low achievers can learn.
- Technology can be used effectively to encourage high quality mathematics learning.
- Students can figure things out on their own and that is stronger learning than if you tell them.

WHAT ABOUT EXEPRIENCED TEACHERS?

Connie called me up one day to ask if I might be interested in working with middle grades teachers in her school district. Connie had been a student in my mathematics curriculum course a couple of summers before I got that call. She wanted to set up an appointment to bring one of her district administrators to discuss classes they wanted me to teach for their middle grade teachers. There was a grant they wanted to turn into distance technology classes. The grant funders were seeking a group to develop content courses for middle grades teachers.

By content, they meant that the main purpose was for teachers to learn more mathematics. After conferring with my colleague, Dr. Cady, we decided that we wanted to develop these courses with two basic tenets. First, the teachers were to become their own mathematical authority, thinking through the mathematics for themselves. Second, we wanted them to learn the mathematics content as a byproduct of focusing on student thinking about the mathematics.

Every step of the way we asked, "What will your students think? What difficulties will they have?" Like a bulldog on a bone, we doggedly maintained the focus of their studies on examining student thinking on particular pieces of content, similar to the Taylor version of a lesson study. The setting for teacher learning in this project was very different for several reasons. First, we were challenged to do most of the coursework with these teachers via technology. Second, these were inservice teachers. They had day jobs. Furthermore, they were also members of a broader community. These were soccer moms and dads.

Holding to the learning framework outlined in the student learning chapters, the key to success and what the teachers claimed was the most important thing was respect. We called it knowing our audience and respecting their context. You understand our lives, you understand us, you were willing to work with us instead of telling us what's what and you got us to think through it on our own. The teachers called it respect. We presented the opportunity to learn. We presented the structure, the reason, the resources, and then we left it up to them. We called it working from their current beliefs and challenging them to ask questions and answer them. They called it respect.

The only thing we did while leaving it up to them was to point them to structure, reason, and resources. As we moved them through various content topics, we continuously refocused:

- We asked, "What makes sense to you?"
- We corrected any misconceptions after that because we did #1 first.
- We required metacognition.

Metacognition is the awareness of and reflection upon one's own thinking. It is revisiting the knowledge (re-traveling the paths), reorganizing thinking patterns to make the most sense (paving), and making sure the teachers realized that they had learned something new and valuable about this middle school content (hitting the save button to capture the image of this new map).

The end results were teachers that knew mathematics better and knew how to support student learning of mathematics much better. Moreover, they knew more about how to take an organized approach to learning from experience.[9] I have heard it said that there are two kinds of teachers that have been teaching for thirty years: those with thirty years of experience and those who have gone through one year of experience thirty times. Without an organized approach and a habit of metacognition, a teacher is likely to fall into the latter category.

AUTO-SAVE FOR STUDENTS AND TEACHERS

Metacognition is a powerful tool for fortifying the knowledge (cities) and strengthening, renewing, and paving the connections (roads) constructed in natural learning. In the interest of moving students towards autonomy, the best thing we can do for them is encourage them to pick up the habit of ongoing metacognition. If metacognition is like hitting the save button when typing something on a computer, then the habit of ongoing metacognition is like having auto-save. Auto-save is that feature that keeps saving your work as you go so that if your computer shuts down before you save your document, you will not lose it all. All of the best thinkers in the world have the habit of ongoing metacognition. This auto-save feature is also one of the fundamental ingredients in the idea of transfer, successfully applying old knowledge to new situations.

Nearly without exception, people believe that teachers should model good behavior. They demand this in terms of morals but we have not yet demanded that they model learning as they are teaching. They are required to learn via professional development projects, special teacher workdays, and almost all teachers end up with at least a master's degree. These, however, are not things the students see. If a teacher is a model of lifelong learning but never exhibits it in front of a child, what impact have they made on the children's beliefs about learning? They need to model the natural learning process, which is, of course, natural to the act of teaching. They choose a pedagogical problem (how to encourage student learning of a particular content), gather resources and information to solve the problem, work with colleagues to solve the problem whenever possible, and carefully analyze the results. Whether it is a lesson study, a minor research project, or implementing a new curriculum, teachers should be constantly learning and discussing their learning process with the students.

A Word to Teachers – It is a common occurrence in our profession to attend a workshop that is really powerful and to go back to our own setting with no idea of how we might implement it in our school, with our students, or in our curriculum. If you want to overcome this, here are some simple suggestions:

1. You are not alone so don't act that way. Even if you are the only one in your school, district, or county that wants to try something out, there are plenty of teachers that would love to do it with you. In the information age, we are never alone. Use collaboration tools such as email, texting, video-conferencing ... you get the picture. You may even go old-school and use a phone.

2. Go about it in an organized way. Treat your assessment information like data because that is what it is.

3. Carefully examine all of the questions in the framework in chapter 5 as you plan your lessons, as you implement your lesson, and when you evaluate its impact on students.

4. Think about your thinking. Reflect on what you were thinking in each stage of the project and how that might have impacted the learning.

5. Share the results. Present it at a local conference. Other people want to hear about your experience and learn from it.

CHAPTER 7:
NATURAL SCHOOLS

As we have seen, standardization and the assembly line have influenced the structure of schools. As a general rule, the structure of schools has influenced how students and teachers tend to think about their jobs and the content for which they are responsible. What about the best and brightest? Are the most outstanding teachers prone to this compartmentalization?

I had the privilege recently of inviting the movers and shakers of mathematics and science education in the great state of Tennessee to a meeting. Most of the invitees were professors, department chairs, and deans from colleges who were done with their semester. The rest of the participants were K-12 teachers and administrators at the district level.

Although there was little funding and no promises of support in the future, almost everyone that was invited chose to participate. They came because they wanted to work together to improve education in our state.

Not only was this group of people special because of their desire to improve things for children, but they were also highly motivated to act immediately. Throughout the meeting, two or three would start to collaborate and solve some of the problems we were facing. Each time I saw this occur, I asked them to stop. The shocked looks on their faces communicated their message to me very clearly: "Why? You invited the movers and shakers and here we are moving and shaking. Isn't that what you want us to do?" Man, were they frustrated with me! They love solving problems and that is what they do. They solve problems. They are good at it. Really good. What we needed, however, was a fundamental shift in our culture. Rather than solve the symptoms, the immediate problems like teacher shortages, we needed to solve the actual problems: our expectations of ourselves, our norms for how we operate. A few of us had decided that we had had it with watching effective people work on the same problem in different compartments, with little knowledge of the work of others.

Although I am certain that I have missed a few organizations, I know that we had representatives of:

- Tennessee Mathematics Teacher Association (TMTA)

- Tennessee Science Teacher Association (TSTA)
- Tennessee Association of Mathematics Teacher Educators (TAMTE)
- Tennessee Science Education Leader Association (Tn-SELA)
- Tennessee Council of Supervisors of Mathematics (TCSM)
- Tennessee Mathematical Association of Two-Year Colleges (TMATYC)

This is just a portion of what I refer to as the alphabet soup of STEM education in Tennessee. STEM stands for science, technology, engineering, and mathematics. Politically and as a practical reality, STEM education is tremendously important because of the technological direction our world has taken. Regardless of their position as leaders in STEM education, until we were sure that everyone actually understood the real problem, our culture, we wouldn't let the movers and shakers solve one single problem.

If we had set them loose from the beginning of the meeting, there would have been a lot of positive results. As a result of making them wait, however, instead of having several small projects merge into larger projects we did something very different. What we managed to accomplish was the creation of a council with representatives from all the different kinds of STEM educators, people whose job it is to improve the teaching of mathematics and science. We committed to work together as a group, to communicate, and collaborate as we work toward our common goal. What we created at that meeting was a shift in the culture, an increase in communication and an increased likelihood of collaborative problem solving which steps outside of our usual compartments of thinking and operating to make a bigger difference.

What if we did that as a nation to focus on the cultural problems undermining the work of our schools? What if the alphabet soup of education met to rethink the purpose, structure, and implementation of education in America? Even the idea of having schools is up for rethinking. Why do we congregate our children and treat them like automobiles? Why are we serving them education's version of the greasy cheeseburger instead of a balanced diet of natural food that they collect and prepare? What might education look like if we organized around different assumptions? What assumptions should we make on which to base all ideas, structures and processes of education in America?

Let's revisit the fundamental ideas of natural education:

1. Learning is an adventure and should always be presented that way.
2. Learning should be based on problems that the students have a need to solve, through experiencing the problem, making sense of

the information, and communicating a solution.

3. Practice and memorization come after initial learning of that content. Moreover, practice and memorization come through continually solving new problems rather than practicing the same problem repeatedly with slightly different information.

4. Advancing in the American educational system should be based primarily on mastery of concepts and skills rather than on age and the passage of time.

5. Assumptions 1 through 4 apply to the learning of all of those involved in the formal educational process: students, parents, teachers, administrators, and the policy-makers.

Assumption 5 is particularly important. If we only consider the natural learning of the students in redefining and restructuring public education in America, then we will most likely end up with another faulty system. Do not leave the senators and the president out of the loop or we will end up with another No Child Left Behind incident. Just like the structure of schools, NCLB was the right idea defined and implemented the wrong way. (More on that comes in the next chapter.)

If public education in America were based on these five assumptions, what might it look like? This is obviously too big of a question to be answered by only two teachers (the authors) but I would like to pose one idea to simplify the matter a little. I would like to suggest that the best way to reorganize education in America is to focus on teacher learning as the highest priority, the central tenant of the system. I do this with one caveat: teacher learning must be focused on student learning. Just as in the lesson study and research projects we mentioned in the chapter on teacher learning, the system should be based on teacher learning which is based on the collaborative examination of student learning. Everything that happens in schools would be based on organized investigations of empirical data generated by students. Teachers, schools, systems, and policy would change as student data changed. It would be like one huge collection of ongoing investigations, like a marathon of detective shows on television. The collective adventure of improving student learning and achievement in America!

EDUCATION IS A TEAM SPORT

Since we are all stakeholders in education, we share in a collective responsibility for changing the schools to support natural student learning. Hence, we must encourage collaboration amongst those stakeholders. Collaboration among teachers is a lofty goal but collaboration among all stakeholders is what we are after. The highest form of collaboration is collegiality, working together (not in separate silos) on a joint project with shared goals.

Collegiality among teachers has four attributes:[10]

(1)   Professional trust. Trust that you know your subject, know how students learn best, and have the students' best interest in mind.

(2)   Expertise sharing. Everyone has something to share. At the highest level, there is mutual sharing of ideas, techniques, and

(3)   Collaboration. Not only are the teachers working together, but there are mutual contributions to shared problem solving.

(4)   Accountability. Everyone on the team believes that they are responsible for every student, regardless of whether they will ever be their teacher. In terms of teaching there is a simple dichotomy: are these *my* students or *our* students?

In the best teaching environments, the leaders encourage all four of these attributes. The great thing about collaboration in a natural education setting is that these four attributes tend to take care of themselves. Do you remember what happens in bike riding? The need to solve the problem eventually outweighs the risks. So it is with professional trust. The more motivated a teacher is to solve a problem, the more likely they are to throw caution to the wind and trust their peers. This is a byproduct of having the teachers focus on a problem that is meaningful to them and giving them the time and resources to solve it together. Expertise sharing is also a byproduct as teachers engage in a continual cycle of problem solving. Eventually all of the teachers participating in the sharing move toward becoming experts. Their passion for student learning and their sense of collective responsibility outweigh their insecurities and they talk about what they know.

The increases in trust and expertise-sharing pour out into mutual contributions toward solving the problem. All of the elements exist but they exist only in a natural learning situation. When teachers are required to solve problems which they do not see as a priority, however, the learning is unnatural. In this contrived collaboration, all four of these categories of collegiality come crashing down. When I decided the questions to be answered in my teacher education courses, I used to have my students, future teachers, come to me regularly saying, "I can't work with this group. This person is being lazy!" In implementing a more natural education situation where the students help to define the problems that we solve, collegiality abounds. While there are still groups in which some people carry more of the burden of the work than other people, I am not getting those complaints anymore. Since I have made sure that the key assignments they do are work that they define (with guidance from me), then the problem of establishing and supporting collegiality solves itself by simply asking them to refocus on the task at hand.

CHANGING AMERICA TO SUPPORT LEARNING

How then, are we to organize the work of educating people in America? Organized around teacher learning, around 50% of the teacher's time at school would be given to interaction with students, guiding their learning. The other 50% would be dedicated to analyzing the student data, getting input from colleagues, solving school-wide issues, and planning for instruction. The impact on students would be tremendous and positive. Teachers' time with students in this environment would be twice as effective as the impact that they currently have on students because they had the time, the resources, and the input from colleagues that they need to have such an increased effectiveness.

This, of course, has a tremendous effect on our systems. If only 50% of teacher time is spent with students, what does that mean? Does that mean that students are unsupervised for half of the school day? Of course not! Does that mean that we need more teachers? Maybe. Does it mean that class sizes increase? Maybe. With a more effective approach, maybe the larger class size would not have the same negative effect that it does in our current system. One certainty is that states ought to require that the school year and school days are structured in ways that support learning as opposed to the way they are currently structured. Most teachers have little time to ask the questions they need to be great teachers.

In order to accomplish this restructuring, we need to get away from the babysitting approach to school scheduling. We should **not** determine the schedule for learning by convenience of the people who are neither students nor teachers. On the chopping block for possible expulsion are such items as the agrarian model, no school in the summers because students are needed to work the fields, and the work-week model, which is more about the convenience of the parents than it is about their children. Maybe students only go to school for half the day. Maybe students have time where they are supervised by teaching assistants.

Perhaps we could go to a four-day week where Wednesdays are days for teachers to investigate how students learn and plan accordingly and do joint research. We could hire twice as many teachers with teachers only teaching half as much, thereby

> Teachers would move away from "grading" and move towards data analysis reporting.

allowing them a full half of their structured workday to be learners. We know this is incredibly expensive and totally impossible in most people's minds, yet I would conjecture that it would solve nearly all the problems in American education. Teachers would move away from "grading" and move towards data analysis reporting. They would have the opportunity to regularly refine their lesson plans based on their careful, ongoing, collaborative research that utilizes the framework for learning described in chapter 5.

In the present structure, an elementary school teacher may teach 7 lessons each day, 5 times each week for a total of 35 different lessons. To study each one of those lessons carefully means they would likely never fully explore and research each lesson, particularly if the curriculum shifts with any regularity. This is obviously not a structure in which a careful focus on the learning of each child in each lesson is supported.

Why does it make sense to restructure everything? Can we not hire a group of teachers to work things out and have other teachers learn to apply the lessons? The answer is the same as it was in the beginning of the book. To have some teachers learn naturally and the others merely accept their thinking is another unnatural case of prepackaging knowledge and delivering it. It is the fattening of the teacher's mind. Because they didn't do the work, they don't *own* the knowledge and don't understand the nuances of the student difficulties. Because they didn't do the work, they haven't analyzed the pitfalls, the strengths, the important attributes of the big ideas and how the students learn them or don't learn them. It is never good enough for a committee to do the tough work for the teacher. Teachers need to be active learners so we can't ignore their need to learn anymore than we can ignore the need to learn on the part of the student. We can't expect them to be "good" if we define good as "active learning." Teachers are learners and need to be treated as such.

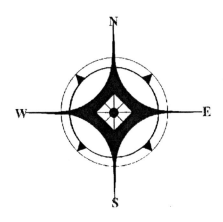

CHAPTER 8:
HOW DO WE GET THERE?

As we wrap up this book, there are still two democrats actively seeking their political party's support to run for president in the 2008 election. After eight years of George W. Bush in the White House, what is the battle cry of all Democrats? CHANGE! Whichever side of the line you may happen to be on, it is clear that we could use some change. The economy is in recession, we remain at war abroad, and foreign companies seem to be gradually taking over America. Some changes are occurring whether we want them to or not. Did you know that there are more than five times as many words in the English language as when Shakespeare was writing? Thousands of new books are published every day.

The information age is upon us and we increase our capacity to send and receive information three-fold about every six months. It has been said that,

"...the top ten jobs that will be in demand in 2010 did not exist in 2004. We are currently preparing students for jobs that don't yet exist; using technologies that have not yet been invented in order to solve problems we don't even know are problems yet."[12]

There is good news about schools in America! There is a move toward a cycle of renewal based on data. Schools, districts, and states are all working diligently on trying to institute this kind of system. The bad news is that the current structure of schools does not support those efforts the way that would be needed to encourage natural learning. As Stigler and Heibert point out in The Teaching Gap[8], America's schools are not designed for change.

All of the many calls for change in our schools can be placed into three categories of solution strategies:

1. Panic and keep trying to meet adequate yearly progress requirements of NCLB.
2. Actually implement "research-based" teaching.
3. Call for a Redo.

SOLUTION STRATEGY #1: PANIC

We know that the panic strategy by itself is ineffective. As we said earlier, the No Child Left Behind legislation had the right idea behind it but was poorly implemented. It is basically the political equivalent to yelling at the schools to change without doing anything to actually support that change. NCLB should have been an education bill: educate the public, educate the legislators, educate the administrators, educate the teachers, and educate the parents. I once saw a sign at the back of a classroom:

> Life is a test.
> It is only a test.
> Had this been an actual life,
> you would have been given
> better instructions.

This sums up any attempt at changing education in America that has been made up to this time. Had this been an actual attempt at change, there would have been a lot more planning, a lot more funding, and a twenty-year deadline to meet. Twenty years may seem like an eternity to wait but there are research-based strategies from the 1940's that have yet to be fully implemented in schools. Project 2061 from the American Association for the Advancement of Science actually set a 72 year goal for changing education. Twenty years would be record-setting change. Since the NCLB yell-louder and threaten approach has been implemented, surface-level change has taken place but nothing of significance. There are still plenty of schools in panic mode.

SOLUTION STRATEGY #2: ACTUALLY IMPLEMENT "RESEARCH-BASED" TEACHING

A Natural Question: A colleague of mine was attending a conference in Sweden. In the middle of a conversation on educational change and mathematics pedagogy, the comment was made, "The reason that our country (Sweden) scores better in international comparisons is because we implement much of the wonderful research done by people in your country. Why don't your schools implement that research?"

I know that this must seem like a no-brainer to most folks, but it is not as easy as it seems. Although educational research has come a long way in the past thirty years, the dominant pedagogy remains the behaviorist approach of a clear explanation and copious amounts of practice. Like the good folks of Anatevka, we are all greatly influenced by tradition. For many, the reason they became teachers was because they were among the minority of students that actually enjoyed the academic aspects of school. They did well enough in the old system and see no need to change. This, however, disregards the high number of students that did not fare as well, that did not thrive in school, and the many who did not reach graduation.

That is not to say that certain teachers, schools, and systems have not made important changes. I have witnessed a great many cases of advanced pedagogies based on research that have shown themselves to be much more effective than rote memorization and stimulus-response. Unfortunately this is more the exception than the rule. Hence, tradition marches on nearly unchallenged.

Beyond tradition, there are the failings of the establishment: those who oversee the world of education but rarely have any expertise in it. The No Child Left Behind (NCLB) legislation is the most prominent and influential example of this. The idea of accountability in education is great. The idea of checking in and making sure that students are making "adequate yearly progress" is highly critical. It is in the practical details of the legislation that NCLB falls to pieces. Have you ever looked at the entire No Child Left Behind legislation? I once printed the table of contents for the NCLB document. In a tiny font barely readable to anyone over the age of forty, it was 19 pages. That was only the table of contents!

Teachers have learned a great many things from NCLB. The first is that the government does not care about them. NCLB raised the blood pressure of every teacher in America, regardless of how effective and successful they might be. Jobs are at risk. Schools are at risk. What support and guidance has been given through No Child Left Behind? In the attempt to influence what people do, one should recognize it as an opportunity for natural learning:

- seek to understand the system in which those people work
- decide who needs to change
- decide how you want them to change

- figure out how to communicate with them effectively
- convince them of the need to change
- support them as they seek to change; this includes technical support, logistical support, financial support, and emotional support
- recognize their efforts and celebrate the change

There is little evidence that any one of these steps was attempted with the vigor and effort which would enable the legislation created to be effective. Rather than encouraging significant learning that will have a positive impact on the future of our students and our country, No Child Left Behind has had the opposite effect. Instead of sending the teachers in the direction of natural learning, No Child Left Behind has sent teachers running in the opposite direction. They need quick results. One of the results is a movement toward teaching only the content that is tested. Since processes are difficult to measure, the tests tend to be full of stimulus-response questions: when you see this kind of question, you always do this exact procedure or write this exact answer. *Don't think, just do.*

As a result, the teaching and learning occurring in classrooms across America is moving that direction, back toward less thinking and more basic skills. Unfortunately, what most people mean by basic skills is low-level thinking which consists of memorizing facts and procedures. In the language of the brain as a road map, the focus on basic skills and the stimulus-response format is like setting kids in the middle of a dense forest, showing them two locations (the stimulus and the response) and having them run the path until they are exhausted. This clears the path for a while, but it does not pave it. The path stays clear as long as the students continue to frequent the path. This explains the several weeks of review that most schools engage in before the state test. The students need to travel a lot of paths a lot of times to make sure they are clear enough to help them do well on the test. What the schools are failing to realize is that if the students had learned the content in a natural way, the paths would be paved. This means that very little review would be needed.

The latest signs of flailing from our nation's capital come from the final report of the National Mathematics Advisory Panel.[11] Although many intelligent, well-meaning, and knowledgeable people were on the committee, the end result of their work is fatally flawed in its conclusions on instructional practice. One of the main mistakes in the process that the committee undertook was their definition of high-quality research on which they were to base their results. Their definition of high-quality research failed to include studies that would consider natural education. It is a classic case of supporting tradition and excluding that which is non-traditional. This was not necessarily the intention of the subcommittee, but it was the effect. Since the vast majority of teachers are still teaching in the traditional, unnatural, behaviorist mode of stimulus-response, it would be nearly impossible to create a study that could prove its efficacy by comparing a large sample of those engaged in natural education and those who were not.

Furthermore, it would most certainly not be possible to randomly assign teachers to teach in natural education mode because it takes years for teachers to understand natural learning and teaching. By defining high-quality research as having those two qualities, a large sample and a randomized selection process, the subcommittee excluded the idea of natural education, learning by experience, from being considered by the National Mathematics Advisory Panel. In other words, because it is not widely practiced or easily adopted, natural education could not be considered.

This is not to say that the conclusions in the final report are wrong. They are merely missing some critical facts. If Twain were still around, he might claim that they were missing the most critical fact of all. If this report steers the instructional practice of the next generation, his definition of education will remain valid: Education is what is left over when you forget everything your teacher made you memorize when you were in school.

From the educational research committee, the lesson to take away from the report of the National Mathematics Advisory Panel is this: we need to do more careful comparisons of the methods that we do know to work well. We need to build the number of teachers that understand and apply the principles of natural education to the point where we could do a valid gold-standard randomized study comparing the results of learning content and processes through experience (natural education) to the results of teaching the same content through explicit instruction (unnatural education). Until this is accomplished, the implementation of research that is recognized by policymakers will be limited to doing an excellent job at traditional, stimulus-response teaching.

As it stands, moving toward natural education by the implementation of current research could only occur as a grass roots movement. It would be teachers engaging in the study of their own work, working together on lesson studies, rebuilding American education from the ground up. If you trust your local teachers to think their way through it and find the ways that work through their own natural learning process, then step up and find a way to support them in this effort.

SOLUTION STRATEGY #3: CALL FOR A REDO

Go back to your childhood days for a moment and recall the protocol for situations when the game was absolutely wrecked so much that there was no fair way to continue it. What did you do? In my neighborhood, we called for a redo. A redo consists of restarting the game from the beginning. If it is tag, the person who is "it" has to close their eyes and starting counting all over again. Some people are calling for a redo in terms of income taxes. The tax system is so complex and unfair at this point that they want to start over again with a simple flat-rate system.

This is my suggestion for education in America. Let's call for a redo. Let's go back to the drawing board. Let's start from scratch. Let's do it right this time. Let's demand that our children be given the opportunity to experience a natural education. Let's demand that our teachers be given the opportunity to explore what that means and enable them to do a great job providing that opportunity. Let's have a redo of education in America where kids are as engaged with History, English, and the sciences as they are with video games. Yes, this would be an undertaking of monumental proportions. Yes, this would take years and untold amounts of financial support. There is great risk involved, but we are America. We are the land of innovation and rewarding those that step out of the shadows of tradition and do something new and exciting.

What might this look like in action? This could take many different forms but here are a few structural changes that would definitely be necessary:

1. Restructure expectations for students – Students should move on to the next grade level or course only when they have a thorough mastery of the content as measured by the ability to apply their knowledge in unfamiliar problems/assignments.
2. Streamline the curriculum goals – The National Mathematics Advisory Panel did well by including

this idea. Some call it "focusing on the big ideas." Teaching fewer ideas and skills means more time for each idea, learning things more thoroughly the first time.

3. Restructure the expectations for teachers – The physical structure of schools as well as the structures of the school day, school calendar, and teacher pay scales must reflect the high value that is placed on collaborative teacher learning focused on improving student learning.

This change is going to take a lot of people taking a lot of risks. One thing that we have learned well in education is that broad sweeping changes are rarely effective. The pendulum of education swings back and forth. Old-timers know that if they hang on long enough, this too shall pass. In order to give it a real shot, the changes need to occur on a smaller scale first, and gradually get scaled up as a result of success. When it works in one area, others will be desperate to try it.

It may be smart to try this with a few school districts for a while and work the kinks out there before spreading the model. Those districts would have to be excused from the NCLB data pool and the state tests. It may be smart to start with a fresh group of children. Ideally, each district would take the set of children entering kindergarten and implement the change with that group only. First graders and up would continue in the old structure for the remainder of their education. The kindergarteners and all those that follow, would be educated in the new system. At the end of their 4th, 8th, and 12th grades, however that is defined, the achievement level and intelligence quotient of these students would be compared to a district that is extremely similar in numerous ways, socio-economic level of the students, locale (rural, urban, suburban), and other variables identified as having a high impact on academic achievement. Better yet, take the students as they enter college, graduate from college, and as they enter the work force and compare them to their peers. If the schools held true to natural learning for students and teachers, this scenario would yield enough data to do the kinds of statistical comparisons that are so highly valued.

Based on the other kinds of research and the logic outlined in this book, here is my hypothesis: children that experience a natural education will not only far exceed their peers from a traditional education in terms of traditional measures of academic achievement, but they would also go on to become the dominant leaders in the hallowed halls of academia, the corporate world, and in the political arena as well. Other districts would gradually commit to the change and eventually, the change would be supported in broad and meaningful ways at the state and national levels. If we start now, we might be able to bring things around by the time the Halley's Comet returns, the goal of Project 2061 of the American Association for the Advancement of Science.

To those that say that moving the entire American educational system toward natural education is too big and complicated of an effort to take on, I pose the following questions:

- Which of your children or grandchildren, nieces, and nephews is not worth the time and effort?
- Is the future of your country worth that much money to you?

That's what I thought. Grab your trail-blazing gear, America. It's time to take chances, make mistakes, and get messy!

End Notes
---

1   Ms. Frizzle said this on every episode as far as I know. What a great show! As of March 31, 2008, there are still Magic School Bus lessons available from Scholastic at:

www.scholastic.com/magicschoolbus/home.htm.

2   From chapter five of <u>How People Learn</u>, a book from the National Research Council's Committee on Developments in the Science of Learning. (National Academy Press, 2000).

3   From an interview posted on the PBS.org web site which as a part of the work of the WGBH educational foundation:

http://www.pbs.org/wgbh/pages/frontline/ shows/teenbrain/interviews/giedd.html (Page last accessed on March 31, 2008).

4   In his book, <u>Communities of Practice</u> (1998, Cambridge University Press), Wenger extends the notions of Lave and discusses what it means to work and learn in a community. These notions are extremely useful ways of thinking about learning in a culture driven by capitalism. In capitalism, one moves from novice to expert as one uses the system to greatest financial advantage, our definition of success.

⁵ Nearly a century after his study, this is still the
defining work on what it means to be a
profession: Flexner, A. (1915). Is Social Work a
Profession? (Vol. 4). New York: New York School
of Philanthropy.

⁶ The Connected Mathematics curriculum for
middle grades mathematics is an outstanding
example of a balanced approach between
exploration, problem solving, application, and
practice. As of April 1, 2008, the current version
is available from Pearson Education, Inc. at
http://www.phschool.com/cmp2/.

⁷ This is an adaptation of the framework being
developed by a working group of researchers
with contributions made from others at
professional conferences. The core group
includes R. Ronau, P. M. Taylor, B. Dougherty, J.
Pyper, L. Wagener, & C. Rakes. While we put the
final touches on a manuscript to submit for
publication in a professional journal, here is the
reference information for one of the
presentations related to the framework:

> Taylor, P.M. & Ronau, R. (2008, January) "A
> Framework for Studying Mathematics
> Methods Courses" Presented at the Annual
> Meeting of the Association of Mathematics
> Teacher Educators: Tulsa, OK.

8   In The Teaching Gap (Free Press, 1999), Stigler & Hiebert elaborate on the findings of the video study of the Third International Mathematics and Science Study. Since full study never stopped, they have renamed the overall project Trends in International Mathematics and Science Study. http://timss.bc.edu/

9   We are still analyzing the data from this project. Here is the reference information for a recent presentation of our tentative findings:

> Taylor, P. M., Cady, J., & Hodges, T. (2008, January) "Measuring Collegiality in Online Professional Development for Middle Grades Mathematics Teachers" Presented at the Annual Meeting of the Association of Mathematics Teacher Educators: Tulsa, OK.

10   The four attributes of collegiality were defined in a presentation referenced below. This work represents an extension of the work of Judith Warren Little begun in the early 1980's.

> Angelle, P. & Taylor, P. M. (2008, February) "Contextual Catalysts: Preparing Principals to Support Teacher Collegiality" Presented at the Annual Meeting of the American Association of Colleges for Teacher Education: New Orleans, LA.

[11]   National Mathematics Advisory Panel.
        <u>Foundations for Success: The Final Report of the</u>
        <u>National Mathematics Advisory Panel</u>, U.S.
        Department of Education: Washington, DC, 2008.

[12]   <u>Did You Know Video</u>: Karl Fisch
        http://thefischbowl.blogspot.com/2006/08/did-
        you-know.html

Printed in the United States
148336LV00006B/8/P